BANKING THROUGH THE AGES

GRANTING THE CHARTER FOR THE FOUNDING
OF THE BANK OF ENGLAND

BANKING THROUGH THE AGES

BY

NOBLE FOSTER HOGGSON

ILLUSTRATED

NEW YORK
DODD, MEAD & COMPANY
1926

THE VAIL-BALLOU PRESS
BINGHAMTON AND NEW YORK

PREFACE

Back in the pre-historic days when our Aryan fore-
fathers roamed the plains, and when a cow or an ox
was the standard medium of exchange, the crude cattle pens in which these forerunners of our modern
currency were confined became, in effect, the first
banks. Indeed, our own word "pecuniary" is derived
from the Latin word *pecus,* meaning cattle.

Between those primitive cattle pens and the tower-
ing citadels of modern commerce stretches a romantic
story that epitomizes the upward struggle, not of a
calling alone, nor of a people but of human civilization itself. For the pyramids of Egypt, the
temples of Greece, the Street of Janus of Rome, the
palaces of the Medici, all repositories of treasure and
centres of financial activity, were tokens of the development of the artistic impulses and ideals of the nations, but more particularly were they reflections of
the trade, the commercial relationships and the international amities that in our own day find their loftiest
expressions in the magnificent structures that are the
outgrowth of the needs of the great financial institutions of the world.

In this volume the author gives brief but illuminat-
ing glimpses of the progress of banking, told not in

[5]

the academic idiom of the historian but in the informal and casual manner of the banker who is conscious of the spirit of romance with which his calling is imbued.

That the story of banking trails back into the dim mists of antiquity everyone knows. But the fact that this story is replete with intense human interest, with colourful detail, with stirring drama and with a significance to civilization so profound as to be unparalleled in the history of any other vocation, comes to us with a shock of surprise. Yet wars have been declared because bankers have financed them, and peace has been maintained because bankers have withheld aid, and kings and nations and peoples have fought and won and lost because their destinies were decided in the counting rooms. It is with fragments of such a history, told with the vision of a poet who, while treating of the details of his narrative is yet conscious of their larger significances, that this informative volume deals.

Willis H. Booth

FOREWORD

The world tends more and more to organize itself on a business basis. The underlying principles which govern business relationship have proved themselves sound and abiding while political and social systems have changed from age to age.

Perhaps, here in America, the breadth and zest of our business enterprise were absorbed from the stimulating freshness men found in the New World. But the tradition and structure of business were certainly a heritage from the slow and painful development of the Old World.

F. S. Chapin, author of "Introduction to the Study of Social Evolution," says: "Probably no other single force in human history has been more important in bringing about the complete transition from tribal to civil society than the growth of commerce." And this growth began along the borders of the Mediterranean basin where our civilization was born. How long ago may be judged by what is perhaps the oldest commercial record which we have thus far traced. It is the rock-graven story in the Valley of Hammamat, Egypt, describing an exhibition sent by Pharaoh Sankh-ka-ra to trade with the people of the "Land of Punt," which was possibly the Somali coast of Africa on the Gulf of Aden. This was approximately thirty-nine hundred years ago and the commercial organization it implies must have long preceded it.

But it was in Babylonia, rather than in Egypt, that business first developed as an integral factor in the lives of the people. Though Egypt was the mother of most of the industrial arts, the people were so bound to the land and intercourse among them was so restricted that commerce as the fruit of those arts never fully matured.

In the Mesopotamian valley, on the other hand, when the curtain of history lifts, we encounter an economic organization as advanced, in many ways, as it was in Elizabethan England. This is disclosed in the laws of Hammurabi, promulgated in Babylon 2,000 B. C., and in the many legal and business documents from the period of this great king's reign which have come down to us in the form of cuneiform inscriptions on baked clay tablets.

These records, of which there is a surprising quantity, give a fairly accurate picture of what must have been the daily life of the community at that time.

The prosperity of the country depended on the preservation of dikes which confined the waters of the Tigris and Euphrates and the irrigating canals by which the life-giving waters were distributed through

[8]

the fields. A strong administration naturally kept up these important works while a weak and inefficient one let them decay. Because the king was thus the key to the prosperity of the nation he came to control its agriculture and finally all its industries. So, issuing from the king, there were laws regulating the use of irrigation water, the rent of land, grazing, the wages of workmen, the business of the commission men or agents, debts, interest and virtually everything pertaining to the economic life of the realm.

Rent was fixed at about six bushels of wheat an acre. Interest might run as high as thirty-three and one-third per cent. Imprisonment for debt and sale into slavery were legal, but at the end of the fourth year the debtor had to be freed. The wages of skilled workmen were about thirty-five cents a month based on wheat that sold for seven cents a bushel.

There were many slaves, as there were among all conquering peoples of antiquity, but side by side with them worked free farmers, laborers and tradesmen who were permitted within legal limits to exercise their own initiative, to undertake business ventures at home or abroad and to make contracts for the future.

These undertakings are set forth and described in the Babylonian clay tablets. In this enduring form our archeologists have found deeds and leases of land, wills of personal and other property, accounts, notes,

[9]

mortgages, receipts for storage, agreements, and various other business forms which must be considered the progenitors of those of to-day.

Neither need business efficiency be regarded as a wholly modern development. These clay records could be, and were, made in duplicate by the simple process of pressing wet clay over a tablet which was already baked and then baking the wet impression. The process could, of course, be repeated as often as desired, or at least until the original impression was blurred in transfer. These records were stored in the temples or courts in much the same way that our legal documents are at present kept in halls of record.

This general economic system of Babylon was the primal influence, in fact, the direct ancestor of the system developed by Assyria and Persia, as well as by such highly important commercial states as Phœnicia and Lydia. The bare records naturally do not fully disclose the actual practice of business in these remote periods but we know that it resulted in great prosperity. Here and there particular provinces or cities became renowned for their wealth and enormously rich individuals occasionally appeared. One man, for example, is said to have entertained the whole of Xerxes' army.

Directly connected with these prosperous commercial nations but a little out of spiritual touch with the development of their civilizations, were the Jews, later to become the shrewdest of trading peoples. In ancient times Palestine was essentially an agricultural community and for that reason the first business principles of the Jews were an outgrowth of farming or grazing.

One of the most striking of their legal provisions was that land could not be sold in perpetuity, though it could be leased. The date of consummating a lease automatically determined its length, as all leases terminated each jubilee year. A Hebrew could sell himself or his children into slavery, but for no longer than a seven year's period. It was also compulsory to settle or cancel debts at the end of a seven year's period. Workmen's wages had to be paid at the end of the day on which they were earned. Interest was not only illegal but was forbidden by the priesthood, yet it was permissible to take it from foreigners. This provision of Old Testament law was of the utmost importance in that it became the basis of the pronouncements of the mediaeval Catholic Church against usury.

Athens was superbly situated to become a great commercial centre and, driven by the necessity of importing wheat and other food stuffs for her growing population, extended her trade almost to the ends of the then known world. At the time of her supremacy business was closely controlled by the government. Details of administration were largely en-

trusted to commissions and there were innumerable
commissioners. Ten market commissioners saw to it
that articles offered for sale were wholesome and
priced fairly and ten other commissioners looked after
weights and measures. Thirty-five grain commissioners, chosen by lot, fixed the price of grain in the
market, insisted that the millers sell their meal in
proper relation to the price of grain, and that the bak-
ers did not make more than a reasonable profit. Merchants in the seaports tributary to Athens were compelled to bring to the market two-thirds of the grain
imported from abroad. Materially speaking, Athens
was one of the great cities that lived by bread alone.

While private trade thrived in the city, Athens and
all Greece in the Fourth Century B. C., was built so-
cially on a foundation of slave labor. As against
100,000 free Athenians, and another 100,000 free foreigners resident in Athens, there were, according to
Ctesicles, 400,000 slaves. All the great industries,
such as silver mining and the manufacture of armor,
depended on slave labor. Nicias paid their masters
an obol (about three cents of our money) a day for
each of the many hundred slaves he worked in the
mines. The father of Demosthenes, the orator,
owned thirty-two slave sword cutlers, which cost him
more than one hundred dollars apiece but brought him
in a yearly profit of six hundred dollars.

Before the time of Solon slavery for debt among

the citizenry was a general cause of complaint, but the great law-giver, according to Aristotle, freed these people once and for all by prohibiting all loans on the person of the debtor.

Rome after her supremacy presented a new phenomenon in the business world. Before the Roman conquest each of the nations, Persia, Phœnicia, Egypt, and Carthage, was content with her own development and without regard for the growth and extension of International Commerce. And prior to the "pax Romana," that Roman peace of almost 400 years which spread over the then civilized world, the only blending of international interests ever attempted was that brief conquest of the east by Alexander of Macedon and his immediate successors.

In early Rome, as in Greece, slavery for debt was permitted under the law. In 450 B. C. the twelve tables provided that a debtor might have thirty days in which to pay after a judgment had been rendered against him, but, that if he failed to settle, his person might be seized by his creditors. A father was also permitted to sell his son into slavery but after he had done so three times the son was released from paternal control.

Tacitus, the Roman historian, tells us that the twelve tables limited interest to one-twelfth for the lunar year or ten per cent for the solar year but that this regulation was constantly evaded. In 342 B. C.

[13]

mitting that it might even be honourable if conducted in a large way from a country estate and without too much attention to sordid detail. It is not of record that Cicero ever tried to conduct a successful business on this basis.

Senators were still forbidden to enter trade but nevertheless managed to do so through the agency of freedmen and associations. Thus many freedmen rose to wealth under the Empire, and in some cases to power. The government continued to exercise a benevolent control over economic affairs. The edict of Diocletian in 303 A. D. promulgated a long list of what the government considered reasonable prices and wages. Though it probably did not remain long in force it is an important historical document and throws a sharp light on the economic conditions of that period.

But the authority of Rome had already begun to decay. With the fall of the Empire the roads were destroyed, pirates again infested the seas and foreign commerce virtually ceased. Business once more became local and confined to the individual town or district which was obliged to depend largely upon its own resources.

So, as the opportunity for enterprise ceased, the value of interest became obscured. The church, reviving the old Jewish law, forbade any interest whatsoever, though, as a matter of fact, certain exceptions were made in practice. The crusades, those huge enterprises of the church, were financed by loans against pledges, but not at interest.

By the Twelfth Century the guild system had become well established and for the next four or five hundred years European industry was organized on that basis. If a tradesman or craftsman needed a little money he could borrow it from his guild and occasionally the guild entered into operations on behalf of all its members. Thus business was again bestirring itself in a small way.

But as commerce gradually increased in the Italian cities and the Hanseatic towns of Germany, capital came more and more into demand because it could be used at a profit. Loans at interest once more became common, though they were usually in the form of discount or exchange. Yet it was not until after the discovery of America that interest was legalized either in France or in England. Then such a flood of gold and silver overflowed into the Old World from the mines of Mexico and Peru that business was stimulated to a degree where the appreciation of the function of interest was completely re-established. A new business era had set in.

Through all this vast stretch of history the operation of banking can not be better summarized than by H. R. F. Bourne, author of "Romance of Trade," who says: "The banker's calling is both new and

old.   As a distinct branch of commerce and a separate
agent in the advancement of civilization, its history
scarcely extends over 300 years, but in a rude and
undeveloped sort of way it has existed during some
dozens of centuries.   It began almost with the beginning of society."   To-day it is the foundation on
which is being built the great structure of modern
civilization.

NOBLE FOSTER HOGGSON.

CONTENTS

[19]

ILLUSTRATIONS

[21]

ILLUSTRATIONS

BANKING THROUGH THE AGES

BARTERING IN EGYPT BEFORE THE INVENTION OF MONEY

BANKING THROUGH
THE AGES

CHAPTER I

EARLY MONEY AND THE FIRST COINAGE

AS individuals we are grateful enough when
any of our immediate ancestors leaves us a
little money to ameliorate the struggle of this
complicated modern world in which we live. Yet we
seldom stop to consider what a debt of gratitude we
owe that dim, remote ancestry of ours which slowly,
after much puzzled trial and error, evolved the system
of money on which our whole modern world is based.

Money is a symbol. It stands for a thing offered
or a thing desired. It is a standard of value in convenient form and therefore a medium of exchange.
But in the early days when civilization was just beginning to crystallize from barbarism, the things
themselves—cattle, shaped pottery, weapons, woven
cloth or what not—still had to be exchanged directly.
This was barter. And from the clumsiness and difficulty of barter, a clumsiness and difficulty of which
we, with our bills, checks, notes and ever ready change

can scarcely conceive, the invention of money naturally and inevitably developed.

There may have been coined money at an unsuspectedly early date among the peoples of the submerged civilizations of antiquity such as that of the Cretans, which flowered at Cnossos. There are hints of it among the records of the Sumerians of the First Babylonian Empire, in India, and in the half legendary histories of early China. But in the Seventh or Eighth Centuries B. C. virtually the whole trade of the ancient world centring about the Mediterranean basin was being conducted through barter, and the former monetary refinements of lost empires, if they existed, had been forgotten.

Barter exists sporadically in the world to-day, as among the Esquimaux and in parts of Russia where the organization of society has broken down. As late as the middle of the last century the British economist Jevons, at one time assayer of the Mint at Sydney, was able to study the practice in its most primitive form. He cites it amusingly to illustrate the embarrassment of Wallace, the naturalist, in the Malayan archipelago.

"In some of the islands," says Jevons, "where there was no proper currency, Wallace could not procure supplies without a special bargain and much chaffering upon each occasion. If the vendor of fish or

AN ANCIENT BABYLONIAN RECORD IN BAKED CLAY
BROKEN TO SHOW THE DUPLICATE

other coveted eatables did not meet with the sort of exchange desired he would pass on, and Mr. Wallace and his party had to go without dinner. . . . The first difficulty in barter is to find two persons whose disposable possessions mutually suit each other's wants. There may be people wanting, and many possessing the things wanted; but to allow of an act of barter there must be a double coincidence, which will rarely happen. . . . Sellers and purchasers can only be made to fit by the use of some commodity . . . which all are willing to receive for a time, so that what is obtained by sale in one case, may be used in purchase in another."

Almost everything, at one time or another, has been used as this commodity—wampum, or strung shells among our own Indians and the primitive Chinese, tobacco by our early colonists, bottles of trade gin in West Africa, stamped leather among the Carthaginians, iron among the Hittites and the British Picts.

But no matter what form the earliest money took, among our Aryan forbears, from Dravidian India through Doric Greece to pre-Roman Italy, it was curiously associated with cattle. The Aryans were nomadic or grazing peoples, before they gathered into cities, with great herds of oxen, cows, and sheep. Cattle were what they chiefly had to barter for desired luxuries, and so cattle became the customary, and eventually the traditional, standard of value. The Latin word for money, *pecunia,* is derived from *pecus,* cattle.

From time immemorial in India, through the whole Vedic Age (2000 to 1400 B. C.) the cow was the chief standard of value in matters of barter. As the cow is thus mentioned in the Vedas so the ox appears as a unit of value in the Homeric poems. When the direct transfer of oxen was not convenient or desirable among the Greeks or Trojans, Homer tells us, a weight of uncoined gold equivalent in value to an ox was fixed and called a "talent." In such a primitive society wherever precious metals were used as a medium of exchange they were regarded as merchandise—more convenient for exchange in many cases, but not in themselves measures of the value of other commodities. The ox talents, gradually coming more into use, were finally coined with the head of an ox impressed on one side, and came to be called "oxen."

It was usually thus, as a precious metal, that money came into being. Toward the end of the Age of the Vedas in India ornaments for the neck were used as money. The word "nishka," which originally was merely the name of such an ornament, gradually acquired the meaning of money. In some passages of the Sanskrit manuscripts it is impossible to tell

ANCIENT EGYPTIAN BRACELETS USED AS MONEY

whether a neck ornament or money is referred to. The nishka appears to have corresponded to the copper anklets or bracelets used by the Egyptians of the Seventeenth Dynasty (1600 B. C.) as a medium of exchange.

In the Indian Epic period (1400 to 800 B. C.) the word "nishka" had definitely come to mean a gold piece; and a silver "karshapana," or coin, is mentioned in various Buddhist works. Somewhat later, metal pieces begin to appear, marked to show their weight and hence their value. These copper coins, which were the basis of value in India in the Seventh Century B. C., weighed about 150 grains and show by their punch marks that they were struck, not by the government, but by private individuals.

There were also silver coins in India, oblong or square in shape, and apparently cut from strips of metal. They were without inscription except for the rough outlines of natural objects such as the sun, a man, or a tree, which perhaps sufficed to identify the person who issued them. From their shape, no doubt, the writers of South India called these coins "salakas" or dominoes.

Money in Egypt evolved in much the same way. As late as the New Kingdom, which dates from 1600 B. C., there was no coined money. Up to that time the value of commodities, for purposes of exchange, had been stated in weights of copper.

[29]

The copper anklet, previously mentioned in connection with the Indian nishka, weighed a "deben" and was worth about five cents in our money. A deben of silver was valued at about $4.00. A common price for an ox was 120 debens of copper, or $6.00; while a bushel of wheat sold for approximately two copper debens, or ten cents.

The first actual coins in Egypt seem to have come from the Ægean Islands, perhaps through Minoan traders. The first coins struck within Egypt itself were the silver coins made by the Persian conquerors of Egypt (525 B. C.), bearing an owl and flail design.

One other interesting monetary development in the ancient world precedes the period of definite historical coinage—the silver units used by the Babylonians, and probably adopted by them from an earlier Sumerian people who had already established a flourishing civilization around the upper waters of the Persian Gulf. Here the lowest unit was a grain of silver, which weighed about as much as a grain of barley. One hundred and eighty such grains made an ordinary shekel and 360 grains constituted a great shekel. Sixty shekels made a "maneh," and sixty "manehs" a talent. These units suggest the division of the circle into 360 degrees and of time into hours and minutes, both contributions of Chaldean or Sumerian astronomical science to our heritage of culture.

GOD COIN
PERSIA

CRAB OF COS
ASIA

LION'S HEAD OF LYDIA
ASIA

WHEEL OF CHALCIS
GREECE

SOME OF THE EARLIEST DISCOVERED COINS
SEVENTH CENTURY, B.C.

The elaborate mathematical system of the Sumerians progressed by twelves instead of tens, and this system is imbedded in many of our conceptions to-day, especially those involving the division of time.

As early as the ascendency of the Babylonians there is mention of silver being stamped with the image of some god or temple—a device like the later one of the Greeks who used "Temple" as well as other coins. Despite such official impressions, however, the metal coins passed by weight and not by fixed value—in a word, they were still merchandise. In time various shekel pieces came to be cast in half shekel, shekel and five shekel pieces—representing probably the first uniform coinage.

That cast money was being coined by the state in Nineveh may be gathered from graven records of the Assyrian Sennacherib, who thus describes the casting of huge winged lions for the palace:

"According to the commands of the god, I fashioned molds of clay, and poured the bronze as easily as though I were casting half shekel pieces."

This date, about 690 B. C., perhaps fixes the beginning of real coinage, though Gyges of Lydia, whose reign was synchronous with that of Sennacherib's successor, Esarhaddon, is generally credited with having issued the first coins. Herodotus, in

Book I, says: "The Lydians are the first of all nations that we know of that introduced the art of coining gold and silver."

In China the earliest tokens seem to have retained in their very shape the idea of the barter from which they originated. Those of the state of Chi (1122 to 224 B. C.) were in the form of knives, spades, axes, bells and other familiar objects, suggesting that the knife piece was of the value of a knife, the spade piece of a spade, and so on. The knife tokens were all pierced for stringing, as were the shells used in the earliest dawn of Chinese history. Round cast coins, perforated with a square hole in the middle, were introduced in the Chow Dynasty, about 600 B. C., but they were still inscribed as "equal to one axe," one spade, one gong, or one knife. Perforation is still a familiar attribute of Chinese coins.

Thus, through the ages and in all countries which developed a civilization, money of a sort struggled into existence. With the development of the art of casting, coinage passed from its primitive form into something similiar to that which we use to-day.

A GREEK TEMPLE USED IN ANCIENT TIMES AS A
DEPOSITORY FOR VALUABLES

The proportions and details of this building have been used as an
inspiration in designing many modern bank buildings.

CHAPTER II

SACRED SAFE DEPOSIT VAULTS
OF ANCIENT GREECE

"IF a man gives to another silver, gold, or anything else to safeguard, whatsoever he gives he shall show to witnesses, and he shall arrange the contracts before he makes the deposits." So ran the statutes of HAMMURABI as early as 2000 B. C. Thus twenty centuries before the Christian era we find the Babylonians placing their treasure for safe-keeping with trusted men, to whom they paid as much as one-sixtieth of the treasure for that service.

It is true that the Egyptians had what might be looked upon as treasure houses long before this, and even the Pyramids might be considered safe deposit vaults, for in the belief that the soul would live as long as the mummy remained intact, the wealthy Egyptian planned for the safe-keeping of his mummy with more concern than for the most precious of his possessions. With this very personal and distinctly mortuary attitude prevailing along the Nile, it is not surprising that we are obliged to leave this river in favour of the Euphrates to find a practical conception of trust responsibilities.

[33]

From Greece, however, came the real inspiration for the safe deposit department as we know it to-day. Unlike Egypt and Babylonia, both blessed with strong central governments, Greece was divided into many practically independent states and cities which were usually at war with one another or with foreign powers. When not at war they were in a constant state of unrest through the activities of opposing political factions.

By sad experience, or perhaps by happy accident, the Greeks discovered in the Temple the only safe depository which the turbulent times afforded, and which usually remained inviolate. The strong religious principles of the educated classes, as well as the superstitions and fears of the unscrupulous and non-believers, combined to create about the Temple an atmosphere of greater security than could have been attained by any mechanical devices then known.

To the Temples of Greece, therefore, one may look for the first real safe deposit vaults as well as for the beginnings of the functions of our banks of domestic and foreign commerce. On behalf of timid or absent owners, the priests of the Temples received money, precious stones, silver and gold plate, jewelry, important documents, and practically every other form of valuables.

For the safeguarding of treasure there were at first no standard charges made by the Temple banks, but records show that the obliging priests received liberal presents for their conscientious services. Later when the Temples safeguarded valuables as a matter of business, they made regular and substantial charges and the records indicate that they also lent their own funds at interest.

In the history of some of the more important Temples in which the handling of treasure grew into an important activity, one may trace many of the functions of our modern bank. In the Parthenon, for example, and at Corinth, a special chamber called the "OPISTHODOMUS" was partitioned off as a storage vault for gold and silver belonging to the Temple itself and for valuables deposited by the worshippers. In some Temples without such treasure rooms, a portion of the portico was screened off from the central passage for use as a combination safety-vault and museum.

With private bankers as with the smaller Temples where there was no equipment for the proper and safe storage of deposited treasure, such as separate vaults or individual boxes, many mistakes were made resulting in claims which had to be settled by the courts. A typical case is that of a Greek named Timosthenes who left some valuable cups with the best known banker of Athens, a foreigner named Pasion. The banker loaned the cups to a relative to be used at a banquet and they were never returned.

The case was brought into court to settle the value of the cups, and Timosthenes was indemnified.

Inventories of the Parthenon incised on marble tablets show that its storeroom was equipped with shelves and cupboards; various objects are listed as being on the first, second or third shelf or in a certain cupboard.

When the richer Temples at Delphi and Olympia became overcrowded with gold and silver and other valuables, small treasure houses were built within the sacred precincts to accommodate the overflow. Rows of these at Olympia, described by PAUSANIAS, the Greek traveler, were designed like miniature Temples.

Although superstition and religious veneration kept these structures safe from ordinary robbers and sometimes even from raids during violent revolutions, ambitious conquerors and wilful tyrants, now and then, swept aside all such scruples and appropriated the treasures for their own aggrandizement. The Persians during the invasion of Xerxes felt no qualms about the sacking of the great Temple at Delphi. As a matter of desperate necessity it was again looted by the Phocians about 350 B.C. While Dionysius the elder (430 B.C.–367 B.C.) of Syracuse was carrying out his operations against the Carthaginians, he seized from the Temples of Syracuse golden mantels, golden vases, crowns, silver tables, and even the

golden beard of ESCULAPIUS, and having found this
method of securing funds for his campaigns successful, carried the practice into other lands, even allying
himself with the Illyrians for the express purpose of
plundering the Temple of Delphi, in which enterprise, however, he was defeated by the Greek troops.

With the Temple at Agýlla he was more successful,
relieving the Etrurians of treasure valued at 1000
talents, or about one million dollars. Sailing back
from one of these raids before exceptionally favour-
able winds, the graceless plunderer cynically remarked to his friends, "You see how the Greek gods
favour sacrilege."

In those hardy days, even if at intervals some ruth-
less Dionysius resorted to plunder, the rights of property were beginning to be respected and many phases
of the banking business were established on solid
foundations. Nevertheless, despite the atmosphere
of religious awe which surrounded the Greek Temples and tended to keep them inviolate, these treasure
houses of the Hellenes were by no means as efficient
and secure as the average safe deposit vault of to-
day.

"**M**ONEY is indeed the most important thing in the world; and all sound and successful personal and national morality should have this fact for its basis."

GEO. BERNARD SHAW.

CHAPTER III

BANKING DURING THE ROMAN ERA OF PROSPERITY

IMPRESSIVE, indeed, and vividly suggestive of the economic life of the ancients, are the ruins which remain of what were once the banking establishments of the Roman Republic. These offices were situated in a row along the north side of the Forum on the street of Janus, the Wall Street of the time. This locality named after the double-faced God, Janus, is known to have been frequented by bankers and money-changers from the fourth century B. C., although the present ruins are of buildings which date from a period two hundred years later at about which time they were destroyed by fire. When reconstructed they were amalgamated into The Basilica Aunilia, the new courthouse built by Lucius Aeurilius Paulus, overlooking the public square.

The offices were distinguished by numbers on the pillars of the portico outside. There is a reference to one of them in the works of Catullus.

Our sense of the actuality of ancient civilizations is, perhaps, never stirred so strongly as when we look upon the scenes of their every-day transactions. The

Parthenon and the Coliseum fail to give us that feeling of intimacy with the Greeks and the Romans which we enjoy when we see what is left of the less pretentious buildings in which the ordinary business of the day was carried on.

The well-worn marble floors of these rediscovered offices were found covered with loose coins which must have been scattered at the time of a great fire, as many coins have been melted and welded together and cemented to the slabs of the pavement.

An ancient bank consisted of a large, solidly constructed, though sparsely furnished and badly lighted apartment in which the money-changer sat on a high stool with his coins spread out before him behind a bronze mesh screen. His clients entered from the portico in front; now a lawyer to deposit the fee won in the Forum across the way; now a young patrician on his way to the circus, comes to draw a thousand resteatii to bet on his favourite gladiator; now a Thessalian slave to add a little to the growing sum with which he hoped to purchase his freedom.

An American bank teller would speedily have felt at home in these surroundings. We are apt to think of Roman bankers merely as money-changers, forgetting that the broad and complicated commerce of Rome required a banking system of nearly as high a development as our own. A part of an ancient banker's daily routine included the opening of accounts, the

[40]

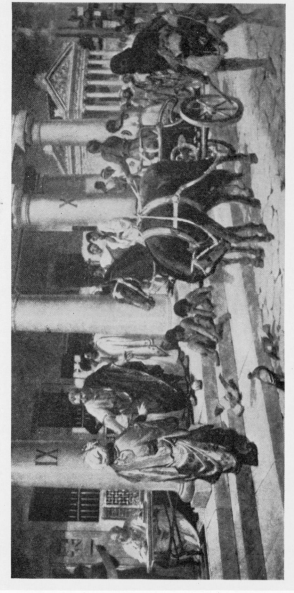

BANKING ESTABLISHMENTS OF THE ROMAN REPUBLIC DURING THE ROMAN ERA OF PROSPERITY

These offices were situated in a row along the north side of the Forum on the street called Janus, the Wall Street of the time

receipt of deposits, the issuing of bills of exchange, the furnishing of letters of credit, the making of loans, the purchase of mortgages; in fact most of the transactions performed by a bank cashier of to-day and his assistants. Interest was paid on time deposits, such deposits being termed credits as distinguished from those which were subject to call, and on which no interest was paid. The sanctioned rates of interest were, at first, high, but decreased in the last days of the Republic until, under the Empire, they were close to the modern rates, two and a half per cent being once recorded.

Judging by the extensive and varied facilities offered to Roman citizens for the safe keeping and the safe investment of the sums of money which constituted the surplus of their yearly balances and savings, it is evident that thrift as well as profitable investment were practiced and encouraged.

Although we have no evidence as to the existence of regular savings banks, we know that money could be put at interest or laid by for future emergencies in three ways: First, by entrusting it to bankers; second, by placing it in the care of priests; and third, by depositing it in safes guarded by the State. In the first case, which was to save the depositor the trouble and danger of keeping the money and making payments from his home, the banker received the deposit but paid no interest. He simply honoured the checks of the client as long as there was a balance in his favour; but when the money was deposited as a *creditum,* that is, for a specified period of time, at interest, the banker was allowed to use and invest it to the best of his judgment.

Ample facilities were furnished by the State for the safe-keeping of money and other valuables. Public repositories were maintained by the government in which the citizens were given the use of guarded safe deposit vaults. The ruins of the buildings used for this purpose, some of which are of vast extent, give a very definite idea of the solidity of the Roman economic system and the secure and firm foundation upon which its wealth was founded.

The true foundation of Roman prosperity was, however, the independence and self-sufficiency of the Roman citizen, and, when these were corrupted and destroyed, the whole superstructure was undermined. When the emperors converted the repositories of the Republic into storehouses for the keeping of grain to be doled out to the mobs instead of providing them with work from which they could earn sufficient to meet their necessities, then the overthrow of Roman rule and prosperity was imminent. *Panem et circeuses* were the forerunners of their downfall.

To a considerable extent the success of Rome sprang from an essential quality which was the thorough and enduring manner in which details were

THE TRIUMPH OF COMMERCE AT OSTIA—HARBOR OF ANCIENT ROME

worked out. The truth of this is strikingly apparent when we study such relics of Roman greatness as we have been discussing. It savours of triteness to say that the Romans built for eternity, yet the words are expressive. The utmost care was given the smallest detail, and construction of a superficial nature was scornfully avoided, whether in the building of a public repository or the organization of a department of the government.

"MONEY which represents the prose of life, and which is hardly spoken of in the parlors without an apology, is in its effects and laws as beautiful as roses."

EMERSON.

CHAPTER IV

COMMERCIAL DEVELOPMENT OF
THE JEWS

WE are accustomed to-day to regard the Jews as a great commercial people with a special aptitude for banking, finance and business of all sorts. But this direction of their genius was forced on them by their evolutionary environment as a homeless and oppressed race.

Until they were driven from their homeland the Jews were probably the least commercial people of civilized antiquity, though they were surrounded on all sides by other Semitic races who had developed business as a fine art. The Jews, however, in the beginning, were nomads who, after settling down in the Land of Canaan, devoted themselves to agriculture in the intervals between their rather unsuccessful wars with the original land-holders, the Canaanites, on the north, and the Philistines, on the south. The Philistines, who do not appear in the earlier stories of the Jews, seem to have been a Mediterranean people who were driven into Palestine when Cnossus, in Crete, was destroyed, 1000 B. C.

The second reference to money in the Bible describes a real estate transaction in which the Jews clearly enough appear as nomads, or tent people, and the Canaanites as town-dwellers. The thirty-third chapter of Genesis tells how Jacob came to "Shalem, a city of Shechem".

"And he bought a parcel of a field where he had spread his tent at the hand of Hamor, Shechem's father, for an hundred pieces of money."

This was undoubtedly the currency of another race for, until the second century B. C., the Jews continued to weigh out gold and silver as payment for merchandise or used the money current in Syria, Persia, Phœnicia, Athens, and the cities of the Seleucidae. Simon, the Maccabee, is said to have been the first to issue the shekel as a coin.

But this is late in the story of Israel. For many centuries the Jews were neither craftsmen nor traders. In I Samuel, Chapter 13, it is stated: "There was no smith throughout all the land of Israel. . . . But all the Israelites went down to the Philistines to sharpen every man his share and his coulter." Hence it would seem that they had not even learned the rudiments of metal working.

Under their third king, Solomon, the Jews enjoyed a brief burst of glory, which has become a tradition of great grandeur, though compared to the magnificence of other potentates of his time it was very limited indeed. Solomon's reign may be set down as some-

THE HOUSE OF AARON OF LINCOLN, AT LINCOLN,
ENGLAND—TWELFTH CENTURY

where around 960 B. C. and its success seems to have been largely due to his alliance with the Phœnicians. This advanced people supplied the Jews with what they lacked, taught them the ways of craftsmanship and commerce, and thoroughly exploited their kingdom as a highway for trade with nations beyond the Red Sea.

When Solomon decided to build his temple he imported Hiram, the worker in brass, from Tyre, to make the brazen vessels and decorations used in his famous monument. In fact the whole impetus toward a wider civilization among the Jews at this time seems to have come from the Kingdom of the Phœnicians. We are told in I Kings, Chapter 9, how Solomon constructed a navy of ships and sent them to Ophir. But this navy, beside the servants of Solomon, was manned by "shipmen that had knowledge of the sea" sent by Hiram, King of Tyre. Obviously the Jews had no previous maritime experience.

Precious metals were also imported into Israel. King Hiram sent Solomon six score talents of gold, together with the timber and metal for the temple and was repaid by the cession of twenty cities together with great quantities of wheat and oil. In the Jewish fleet which the Phœnicians manned, Solomon was later able to bring gold to the amount of 420 talents from Ophir. Though gold was thus brought in there was no coinage in general use until after the overthrow of Jerusalem by the Assyrians.

Indeed, the laws of the Jews were wholly unfavourable to the financing of trade or the development of banking.

In Exodus, Chapter 12, stands the injunction: "If thou lend money to any of my people that is poor by thee, thou shalt not be to him an usurer, neither shalt thou lay upon him usury." In Leviticus, Chapter 25, is found a similar command: "Thou shalt not give him the money upon usury, nor lend him thy victuals for increase."

Such biblical rules as these virtually kept the Jews from banking throughout the early ages and exercised a tremendous influence upon the development of banking in the Middle Ages. Yet the Israelites were crowded in between the Assyrians and other peoples of western Asia, all of whom had legalized the use of interest from time immemorial. It is possible for this reason that in Deuteronomy, Chapter 23, it is expressly declared that "Unto a stranger thou mayest lend upon usury."

This permission was the foundation upon which Jewish banking developed many centuries later. In fact the restrictions against usury may have somewhat broken down even as early as the Roman occupation, during the life of Christ, for in the parable of the unfaithful servant (Luke, 14) we find this question: "Wherefore, then, gavest thou not my money into the bank that at my coming I might have required mine own with usury?" It was a time of the violation of tradition. The Herodian family, ignoring the injunction against graven images, was issuing a coinage adorned with the representation of living things.

Many Jews had begun to leave Palestine. In Alexandria, during the reign of the Ptolemies, there were more Hebrews than there were in Jerusalem itself. And after the fall of Jerusalem, of course, they were scattered throughout the territory of the Roman Empire. It is then that they began to develop tendencies toward trade and commerce as well as toward philosophy, medicine and such other sciences as then existed. Under the Roman Emperors the Jews, with certain exceptions, were compelled to reside in restricted areas. Thus, not having access to the land, they were obliged to turn to trade.

Under the laws of the Roman Empire interest was legal at one per cent a month. As the Jews were expressly permitted by their own laws to take interest from non-Jews the field of money lending was left open to them and they gradually began to specialize in it.

When the Mohammedans swept over northern Africa and Spain the Jews found themselves in the midst of a people whose religious authorities frowned upon interest. Among these also the Jews gradually entered the money lending business, though at first rather timidly and in a small way. There are references to their operations in Alexandria in the Seventh Century, and in Spain soon after the Moorish conquest in the Eighth Century.

Among the Christian countries France, under Charlemagne, was a haven for the Jews. Charlemagne, that great liberal, was unusually lenient for his time and even permitted the Jews to hold land. Louis, the Pious, in the first half of the Ninth Century, was still more kindly disposed toward them and his reign was long looked back to as a golden age.

Meanwhile one synod of the church after another began to take a stand against lending at interest. As early as the Eighth Century there were synodic denunciations of usury and disapproval of lending at interest was established as sound Christian doctrine. This attitude was based not merely upon the Old Testament but upon the statement of Aristotle that "Money in itself cannot grow."

Finally in 1146, Pope Eugenis declared all interest void, and in 1179 Pope Alexander III publicly excommunicated all usurers. The effect of this bull upon the fortunes of the Jews was curious. The excommunication, of course, did not embrace the Jews and only tended to make them still more valuable commercial agents, especially to kings and rulers of

THE FIRST COINED SHEKELS

OF THE JEWS

provinces. Israelites, as a result, became the money lenders for rulers in many lands and districts of western Europe. It was possible for them to lend the money of a prince at interest where a Gentile could not, if he wished to remain a good Christian. It was also possible, and even customary, for the ruler to seize their property after the profits had accumulated.

So useful did the Hebrews become that some monarchs objected to having them converted to Christianity. Both the kings of England and of France demanded compensation for such conversions, and until 1281 the English king declared the property of a converted Jew forfeited to the crown.

One of the most picturesque of these early Jewish financiers was Aaron, of Lincoln. He was born in the city for which he was named some time before 1125 and died in 1186. His financial operations were so wide that he had agents in a number of the English cities. Oddly enough, one of his chief sources of profit was advancing money for the construction of abbeys and monasteries. It was through his accommodation that St. Albans, Lincoln Minster and at least nine Cistercian abbeys were built. At his death these monasteries still owed him equivalent to $24,-000 which, judged by the time, was an enormous sum, as wages were then only seven cents a day.

He also advanced money on houses, armour and

[51]

grain. At his death Henry II seized his property as the estate of a Jewish usurer, devolving by right to the crown. Henry used the cash to wage war against Philip Augustus of France, while the accounts receivable formed a special department in the treasury. Aaron's house still stands in Lincoln and is probably the oldest private dwelling in all England.

The seizure of Aaron's property after his death was typical of the period. Royalty professed to believe that the Jews had no right to wealth gained by money lending and that it was mercy enough to allow them to hold it while they lived. This belief grew into a custom which proved extremely convenient, not to say remunerative, whenever a rich Jew died.

Aaron of York was another English Jew most of whose property, acquired by the practice of interest, went after his death, to the king. He himself stated that he satisfied the demands of Henry III to the extent of 30,000 marks in silver and 200 marks in gold.

A similar sufferer was Ezmel de Ablitas, a wealthy Jew of Navarre. His business of usury was very extensive but he was compelled to grant large loans to the King of Aragon and the nobles of Navarre, none of which he ever recovered. After his death his property was confiscated by the Queen of Navarre on the same grounds urged by other rulers whose excessive piety led them to filch the estates of all Jews who died rich enough for royalty to consider.

"IT is not by augmenting the capital of the country, but by rendering a greater part of that capital active and productive than would otherwise be so, that the most judicious operations of banking can increase the industry of the country."

ADAM SMITH.

CHAPTER V

BANKERS OF THE VENETIAN FLEETS

THE flat mud islands on which Venice stands
were made by the waters of eleven rivers flowing into the Adriatic. Her intricate lagoons
made her a city of asylum and refuge when Attila
drove her first inhabitants before him from the north.
The Adriatic, lapping against her door sills, made
Venice the carrier of Europe's might into the East
throughout the Crusades. And the waters of the
Mediterranean, subdued and controlled by the prows
of her galleys, made her the mightiest city of the continent when Constantinople fell in 1204 and Venice
claimed and received, in her own words "one half and
one quarter of the Roman Empire."

Venice eventually became mistress of the seas, as
far as they were known in the Middle Ages. But
long before that the city had launched upon the maritime career which was to bring such a rich yield.
Never has there been a city where business was more
remunerative or more highly regarded. By the end
of the thirteenth century Venice had become an absolute oligarchy of the wealthier families who formed
themselves into a closed guild for no less a pur-

pose than the exclusive exploitation of the Levant.

Business was more important to many of the Venetians than religion, even in a religious age. As early as 991 Orseolo II had made a commercial treaty with the Mohammedans and a little later, after the conquest of Dalmatia, the city had established control of the Adriatic. Even at that time there was a municipal mint which issued the first reliable coinage of the Middle Ages.

But it was the Crusades which gave Venice her real start along the pathway toward imperial wealth. Throughout the First, Second and Third Crusades, Venice, together with Genoa, her great rival, supplied the transport which moved the armies of the Lord against the Saracens—always at a handsome profit. As a result Venetian settlements began to spring up all over the East. There were Venetian quarters both in Sidon and in Tyre and it is said there were fully 200,000 Venetians in Constantinople when the Byzantine Emperor Manuel stripped them of their possessions and turned them out, precipitating a war with the mother city. To carry this particular war to its disastrous conclusion Venice was obliged to levy a forced loan of one per cent on all net incomes, guaranteeing the loan at four per cent. This was in 1171 and is supposed to be the earliest instance of the issue of government bonds.

When the Fourth Crusade was proclaimed at

THE BANK OF VENICE—SEVENTEENTH CENTURY

Soissons it marked the dawn of the full glory of
Venice. The city agreed to transport 4,500 horses,
9,000 knights and 20,000 foot soldiery together with
provisions for one year at a price of 85,000 silver
marks of Cologne and one half of all conquests.
Dandalo was the Doge at that time and proved himself not only a clever financier but a political and
military genius.

When the time came to move the great army the
Crusaders could not pay. Zara and Dalmatia were
at the time in revolt against Venice so Dandalo
agreed to postpone exaction of the payment if the
Crusaders would undertake the suppression of the
rebellion, which they did promptly. But Dandalo
had only begun his operations. He managed to turn
the whole Crusade against Constantinople, which had
so thoroughly humbled Venice thirty years before.
Largely through his own intrepid leadership the capital of the Byzantine Empire was captured and
sacked. That was when Venice received "one half
and one quarter of the Roman Empire." Venice
was no longer a city. She had become a European
power.

Thenceforth the community became absorbed in
trade. Each year Venice acknowledged its indebted-
ness to the sea when the Doge cast a ring from the
state barge into the waters thus betrothing the city as
the "bride of the Adriatic." Each year the control

of affairs came more into the hands of the great patrician families, organizing themselves for commercial loot. Finally in 1308 all power was concentrated in the terrible Council of Ten. Wars, government, statesmanship—all were directed toward the one ideal of trade expansion.

Naturally, in a city-state organized on this basis, finance and banking had developed as an early necessity. The germ of a state bank was planted in 1160 when the government borrowed 150,000 silver marks from half a dozen of the more important merchants. This was the Monte Vecchio, known as the old debt. Thirteen years later came the forced loan to prosecute the war with Constantinople which added greatly to the government's financial responsibilities.

The right of banking remained virtually free in Venice but does not seem to have been fully used. Before 1300 we read only of *camsores,* or money changers, with benches in the market. Even these, however, made loans at interest. From 1318 there are references to a *bancherius de scripta* which implied genuine bankers who received deposits of money. Thereafter many of the patricians became bankers.

By 1300 the city was already using bills of exchange to send money to its representatives abroad. These were really business agents and made frequent and full reports of commercial opportunities more

[58]

efficient than those of any consular service to-day.

In many cases loans made by the Venetian bankers were a form of bottomry as they depended for security on the prosperous outcome of some venture by sea. The risk being great, the interest was correspondingly high, averaging in the fourteenth and fifteenth centuries, perhaps twenty per cent.

Shakespeare's "Merchant of Venice" reflects conditions on the Rialto at this time, for Antonio's shipping venture furnished the banker Shylock's opportunity for revenge. The Jews, however, were accepted as bankers only on probation, and their licenses were frequently revoked.

Ventures, such as Antonio's, were part of the daily life and business of Venice. Besides innumerable minor voyages to nearby ports in the Mediterranean, great trading fleets were periodically sent out to distant countries. For these the state leased galleys already supplied with arms, ammunition and food and for protection dispatched naval convoys.

The Tana fleet sailed to the Black Sea for trade with the Russians and Tartars; the Syrian fleet sailed to Asia Minor; the Roumanian fleet skirted Greece and penetrated to Roumania; the Egyptian fleet anchored at Alexandria; while the Flanders Squadron sailed through the straits of Gibraltar to trade in Bruges, Antwerp and London. Though the fleets were under government control, each ship was a

[59]

separate venture with its own owner who, in turn, had his private banker.

The *camera,* or bank, which made loans to the government, was receiving about 200,000 ducats in interest at the end of the fourteenth century. By special concession foreigners were permitted to hold stock in the *camera* and it is of record that the Cardinal of Ravenna held 12,000 ducats worth of this stock and the Duchess of Milan 100,000 ducats.

Doge Tomaso Mocenigo declared in a speech delivered in 1423 that the Venetian exports, which covered the "whole world from east to west," amounted annually to 10,000,000 ducats, with imports at about the same sum. The profits on this he calculated at about 4,000,000 ducats, or twenty per cent. As most of this trade was financed by the bankers it is obvious how extended their operations were.

In 1428 the Venetian script outstanding amounted to 9,000,000 gold ducats. In 1482 all the old debts were consolidated in the Monte Vecchio and a new loan of five per cent was placed against special taxes. Various bankruptcies among private bankers in 1502 led to the establishment of a Supervisor of Banks, who had the power to examine the solvency of any firm. In 1525 the city, in order to raise money, began to offer annuities in return for deposits in the mint or, if the depositor preferred he could have perpetual interest at a lower rate.

[60]

ONE OF THE FIRST VENETIAN
COINS, NINTH CENTURY

By a decree of the Senate the first official state bank of Venice was established in 1587. A second institution, the Banco del Giro, known as the Bank of Venice, was founded in 1618, based on a loan of 600,000 ducats advanced to the city by Giovanna Vendarmin.

Both of these banks were without capital and functioned merely as depositories under the management of public officials. They received funds from the state and individuals, charging the latter a stipulated rate. On order of depositors transfers were made on their books and bills of exchange were paid by similar transfer. It was Venetian law that the tender of such a bank credit for more than a hundred ducats could not be refused. It was a basic principle of these banks that their cash or bullion on hand should equal their receipts but, as they were compelled to make loans to the government, they were forced to suspend payment more than once.

Nevertheless the bank prospered when the demands on it were not too heavy. In 1754 interest was temporarily reduced to three and one-half per cent, but in 1766 it was restored to four per cent with a promise to pay depositors on demand.

But all this later bank development constituted mere vestigial remains of financial over-lordship. Venice had long since lost her power and with it much of her affluence. When the Portuguese began

[61]

to sail round the Cape of Good Hope the Mediterranean ceased to be the sole highway to the East. Even before this, exhausting though victorious wars with Genoa, and equally exhausting and losing wars with the Turks had sapped the strength of the state. Yet Venice remained a free city until Napoleon brought the first victorious enemy within its water gates.

The French even burned the famous "Golden Book" in which were entered the names of the great patrician merchants, the hereditary princes of trade and finance. Since then Venice has possessed only a past.

THE PALACE OF ST. GEORGE, GENOA, IN WHICH THE BANK OF ST. GEORGE
WAS FORMERLY HOUSED

CHAPTER VI

RENAISSANCE OF BANKING AND
THE BANK OF ST. GEORGE

FINANCE—what we understand to-day as the power of money and credit—collapsed in Europe with the fall of the Roman Empire. All through the Dark Ages, banking, save as it functioned clumsily through the unskilled hands of feudal bursars, lay under an eclipse.

But along with that extraordinary reflowering of civilization which we call the Italian Renaissance it came to life once more. Indeed, so vigorous was the new commercial growth that in a number of the more splendid Italian civic republics it threatened to swallow the state itself.

Before Columbus opened the highways of the western ocean the Mediterranean, of course, was the great avenue of freighted ships. The cities of the Italian peninsula, which seemed to reach down like a sickle to reap the sea-borne harvest, naturally became thriving centres of this maritime trade. Banking, which early developed as a necessary adjunct of their water traffic, became a passion, then an art, and finally almost a form of government.

[63]

Venice, Florence and Genoa were the chief bene-
ficiaries of this commercial revival and the repositories
of the accruing wealth. The business methods of
all three showed a general similarity, but each developed a characteristic phase of banking. In Florence, for example, banking fell largely into the hands
of great private families. In Genoa, perhaps, banking most nearly approached a public function through
the famous Bank of St. George.

The Bank of St. George, which eventually ruled
a whole broad territory along the north-western
Italian littoral, was at once one of the oldest and
longest lived of the institutions sprung from mediaeval finance. So firmly was it founded, so sagaciously
directed and so tenaciously jealous of its privileges
that it was able to function continuously through
seven centuries. In fact, it may be studied as the
epitome of that system which enabled these tiny
Italian republics, politically so weak they could never
successfully defend their own borders, to finance the
wars of emperors and develop within themselves a
standard of culture unmatched by any contemporary
court of Europe.

The name of the bank itself suggests its mediaeval
origin at a time when all human enterprises, even
those on which the Church looked somewhat coldly,
must have a patron saint. Saint George was that
gallant Roman military tribune in Cappadocia who

became a Christian and for his faith was put to death by the Emperor Diocletian in 303 A. D. His spirit, invoked by the Genoese bankers, is the same ghostly presence which marches ahead of the armies of England and Portugal and is supposed to have swung a doughty blade with the Crusaders against the Turk. In 1101 the fleets of both Genoa and Venice had played a prominent part in reinforcing the First Crusade. In 1147 came the Second Crusade, with the spirit of St. George still leading.

It was only a year later when the initial step in the organization of the bank was undertaken and Genoa contracted her first formal loan. The money was borrowed on future custom duties and the creditors formed a council to protect their interests. Each hundred lire of the debt was called a *luogo,* or share. Any number of shares issued to an individual comprised a column, as they were entered in a book called the *cortulario.* New loans were separately kept. Each was called a *compera* and together they were known as the "Compere of St. George."

Within the next hundred years loans became numerous and their management correspondingly complicated. In 1252, therefore, they were placed under the control of a single corporate body with a chancellor and various other officials. Each loan, as before, was kept separately, with different security and interest. The name "Compere of St. George"

[65]

was officially adopted so that the date, 1252, is often cited as that of the founding of the bank.

Genoa continued to prosper and expand. Loans multiplied right and left. In 1302 it was necessary to call a great assembly which appointed commissioners to draw up 271 articles for the control of the *compere*. One of these stipulations was that the city was thereafter to contract no loan without the sanction of the consuls of the *compere*.

The Bank of St. George operated essentially as a loan bank and in this respect offered a complete contrast to the Bank of Amsterdam. Sometimes the loans were made on curious security. In 1336 Cardinal Fieschi received a loan on the sacred *parossidis*, or holy basin. Although the Catholic Church through the Middle Ages officially frowned on bankers and held interest in any form to be mere usury, this little business arrangement with the Cardinal indicates the beginning of a certain latitudinarianism. In the 15th century the Popes Calixtus III and Sixtus IV formally granted permission to hold shares in the bank. These were a profitable investment, for the bank, in return for loans, received the pledge of the city for its future taxes, or in the case of individuals, the profits of business enterprises. Jewels, also, were a customary form of security.

Like all the Italian mercantile republics Genoa was turbulent. During the revolution of 1339 all

GENOESE BANKERS IN CONFERENCE—LATE
FOURTEENTH CENTURY

the old books of the bank were burned and new commissioners appointed to regulate the *compere*. The city treasury was completely exhausted by building and outfitting twenty-six galleys required in one of the innumerable naval wars and was forced to cede the loot of conquest to the *compere*.

By 1371 more wars and constant internal conflict had utterly destroyed the credit of the city. Francesco Vivaldi, an old patrician, rose before the assembly, and, after explaining the principle of compound interest, gave his shares in trust to the consuls of the *compere* to use the interest on them in buying other shares and the interest on these, in turn, to buy still others. This gift, accumulating as it was bound to, is said to have saved the credit of the state. Vivaldi having shown the way, similar trusts were formed for the maintenance of churches, bridges, fountains and other public improvements.

It was in 1407 that the bank evolved fully into a great public institution. The republic had borrowed huge sums and had assigned various revenues as security. To avoid confusion, all the shares were united in the *compere,* or, as it now became known, the Bank of St. George.

The management was placed in the hands of eight protectors, who were elected annually by the shareholders from a list of thirty-two chosen by lot. Each protector (or director) was obliged to hold shares amounting to 1,000 Genoese florins. This directorate of eight filled the offices of president, treasure general, superintendent for the sale of shares, three judges and two secretaries. The general council consisted of 480 members, elected by ballot, and qualified by the ownership of at least ten shares. It is a striking testimony to the breadth of Genoese business practice that even foreigners were eligible.

The assumption by the bank of state affairs is illustrated in a remarkable floating debt voted by the directors in 1456. As a result of the war against the Turks it was necessary to delay the payment of certain loans for three years. These were listed separately as entered debts to be repaid three years after each matured. By this time the bank had gradually become an independent government within a government. When Mohammed II and his Ottoman army captured Constantinople in 1453 Genoa ceded its Black Sea possessions to the bank. At one time, also, Corsica, Cyprus, and the towns along the Riviera were under the direct government of the bank. Its directorate did not deign to acknowledge allegiance to the city even by so much as flying the red cross of Genoa but proudly unfurled the banner of St. George.

Machiavelli, from his neighbouring retreat at San Casciano, noted the growing power and independence of the bank. Such a successful oligarchy fitted in well with his subtle system of government. In his History of Florence he remarked: "If it should happen that Genoa should fall entirely into the possession of the Bank of St. George, it will then become a republic of greater importance than even that of Venice."

This tendency of the bank to arrogate state powers to itself had been anxiously observed within the city. In 1528 an effort was made to curb it by a law providing that anyone who held an appointment under the government could not hold one under the bank. But as a result of the famine of 1550 the government was forced into a new and supine policy which held the possibility of complete absorption within the bank. In return for a heavy loan it agreed to turn over certain taxes, not merely for a limited period, but in perpetuity. In a word, it sold the people's tax power for the loan.

Throughout this period of growing power the bank had continued to sell shares in different loans, even by auction on the street corners—a scheme which suggests a resemblance to the New York curb market. In 1675, however, the bank ceased these street sales and established four branches in the city. Thenceforth the term *compere* went out of usage and the institution was known exclusively as a bank.

The credit of the organization remained unim-

paired until its gold reserve was carried off by the
Austrian army in 1740. Even then the interest due
was carried as new loans and eventually repaid.
But the death stroke came in 1800, during the French
Revolution. The revolutionaries deprived the bank
of its dearest privilege, the right to receive taxes
which had been pledged as security for loans. This
was its chief source of income. Shortly after the
passage of this fatal decree the Bank of St. George,
which dated its beginning from 1148 and had, at the
height of its influence, exercised all the functions of
a principality, closed its doors for ever.

LORENZO THE MAGNIFICENT, PINNACLE OF THE
FAMOUS FAMILY OF THE MEDICI

CHAPTER VII

THE FLORENTINE GUILD AND THE
BANK OF THE MEDICI

IN 1252 the bankers of Florence, acting through an already well organized guild, issued the first gold florin. It was a handsome coin, displaying on the obverse a lily and on the reverse an effigy of John the Baptist. But more important than that, it was an honest coin and instantly rang true among the various and somewhat dubious currency on which the world then depended. In other cities of Italy, in France, Spain and even Germany, the florin rapidly became a standard of value because it was dependable in weight and pure in quality.

In 1492 died Lorenzo, the Magnificent, pinnacle of the famous family of the Medici. Florence, richest of the renaissance cities, was richest of all, perhaps, in great names—Giotto, Michel Angelo, Andrea Pisano, della Robbia, Leonardo da Vinci, Machiavelli, Vasari, Boccaccio, Tasso, Galileo. But all the dazzling qualities of the city seemed to flower in the illustrious name of Lorenzo, banker and Maecenas.

[71]

Between these two dates, each typical of a period, Florence became not only the wonder city of Italy, but the financial, artistic and intellectual capital of Europe. Only Athens in the age of Pericles can be compared to Florence in the time of Lorenzo. And as for the eminence of the Medici in finance, nothing quite like it had been heard of in the world before. But curiously enough, Lorenzo died in the very year of a discovery that was inevitably to shift the tide of progress westward and change Florence from a world capital once more into a provincial centre.

The Medici, like most of the great families of the city, were bankers and members of the bankers guild, which had produced other financiers of continental calibre in the Bardi and the Peruzzi, while the Medici were still struggling for a commercial and political foothold. The bankers, fourth of the seven great guilds, which through their representatives largely controlled the city, was as exclusive as it was inclusive. No man, no matter what his connections, could bank in Florence unless he was a member and had served an apprenticeship with the guild.

The bankers guild was a very ancient and honourable society. As far back as 1204 the consuls of the guild of bankers and money changers appear, along with the consuls of the other guilds, as signatories to the treaty with Sienna. Records of this interesting

COAT OF ARMS OF THE MEDICI

Today the only survival of the famous Bank of the Medici is the familiar sign of the three golden balls displayed above pawnbroking establishments, an adaptation from the six red balls on the gold field of the Medici shield and the guild shield with its red field strewn with eleven gold florins.

organization are still extant. They reveal in detail the mediaeval formula for creating a banker.

If a boy wished to enter the guild he first signed the matriculation roll and then submitted to an examination before the consuls. The aptness and capacity of the candidate were, of course, taken into consideration, but five qualifications were regarded as absolutely essential. It was required of him to be a native of the city, to have two sponsors, never to have been arrested, to be himself a property owner (or heir to property) and to have paid the state tax. If he was accepted an entrance fee was exacted, which varied from time to time but was always comparatively high.

The fledgling banker remained an apprentice for from five to seven years. During this probationary period his wages were never more than ten lire a year, but his board and lodging were found for him. If he proved a satisfactory apprentice he was advanced to a clerkship in which he was supposed to acquire additional knowledge for another three years before he was permitted to set up in business for himself.

Members of the guild had the exclusive right to favoured locations in the market, such as those in the Mercato Nuovo or along the Via di Tavolini. The outfit of the guild money changer and lender was a simple one—a chair and table for his convenience and

[73]

a green table cloth as the official and protected insignia of his trade. A daybook of ordinary paper, a few sheets of parchment and a balance for weighing coins completed his office paraphernalia.

His stock of gold coin he carried in a pouch fastened to his girdle. Silver for small change was kept in a bowl on the table. It was customary, certainly in the earlier days of the guild, to test both gold and silver by weight, though the florin, worth about $2.40, was presumed to be standard.

Under the rules of the guild members were compelled to keep books which were open to the inspection of its officers. It was also required that these accounts be kept legibly in Roman figures without capitals or special punctuation. The new-fangled Arabic notation, lately introduced from Spain, was not acceptable.

Up to the time of the Medici books were kept on the single entry system, but there were duplicate sets and the daybooks were copied into master ledgers. These were stoutly constructed with leaves of parchment and clamped and locked bindings. Such master ledgers, of course, were retained at the offices of the guild. A general balance was struck once a year and at the same time the value of coins and rates of interest were officially fixed.

Interest was very high and, according to our standards, simply crushing to the debtor. The disapproval of the church seemed to make little difference. In 1427, for example, according to the ledger of Bardi and Piccioli, the interest on 2,928 lire was 878 lire, or almost 30 per cent. Apparently the legal rate was based on what the traffic would bear. But the guild itself seemed to be conscious of the exorbitance of these exactions, for three years later it forbade its members to charge more than four denari a month. As this rate, however, amounted to 20 per cent a month, the bankers still remained fairly well protected.

Many of the terms of the Florentine bankers have come down to us and form a substantial part of our own financial glossary,—*cassa,* for instance, as cash; *banco* as bank; *giornale* as journal; *debitore* as debtor; and *creditore* as creditor.

The headquarters of the guild long stood in the Mercato Nuovo. This splendid building was a monument to the prosperity and culture of the city. Its ceilings glowed with many-coloured murals by the most distinguished Florentine artists and its walls were hung with rich tapestries and pictures in the then newly discovered oil paints as a background for exquisite Florentine sculpture and the marvellously wrought furnishings of the period. The opening and the closing of the city's business day hung upon the toll of the great bell in the bankers guild.

It was inevitable that a system so well organized

and perfected should develop international banking on a large scale. As early as 1260 the guild had begun to issue letters of credit through the individual bankers and funds were sometimes sent as far away as Jaffa, or Tana, on the Sea of Azov.

There were two great eras of international banking in Florence. The first centred around the Bardi and Peruzzi who were, in their time, the supreme financiers of mediaeval Europe. In the 14th century the Bardi established agencies as far north as England and Germany and as far east as Rhodes, while the 130 agencies of the Peruzzi extended from London to Constantinople.

Both houses advanced huge sums to Edward II and III of England, and to the King of Sicily, and both were thrown into bankruptcy when the English King and Parliament refused to repay £700,000 and the King of Sicily defaulted at about the same time.

It was not until the rise of the Medici that Florence recovered from this blow. Banking had been the profession of the Medici for a long time but the first of the family to attain pre-eminence was Giovanni de Medici. Giovanni was born in 1360 and as a young man went through the regularly prescribed steps of an apprentice in the bankers guild.

As Giovanni rose to wealth and power he left his green-covered table in the market place and built

LOGGIA DEL MERCATO NUOVO
Built by G. B. del Tasso, 1547, especially for the money changers
and used by the bankers in the days of the Medici.

himself a palace in the hall of which his main business
was conducted, though he had branch banks in a
number of Italian cities. These bankers' mansions
were a feature of Florence and gave the names to
many of the principal streets such as the Peruzzi,
Tornabucai, Albizzi, Greci, Bardi and Cerchi.

Perhaps Giovanni's most successful venture was
during the council of Constance, from 1414 to 1418,
when he cleared a fortune. In 1429 his estate was
reckoned at 180,000 gold florins, or $450,000 which at
that time had an enormous purchasing power. As
Machiavelli phrases it: "He died exceedingly rich
in money, but still more in good fame and the best
wishes of mankind; and the wealth and respect he left
behind him were not only preserved but increased by
his son Cosmo."

Cosmo remained a banker, conserving and developing his patrimony into another great fortune. But
he enjoyed an even wider success in politics and became, in effect, the dictator of Florence, though he
made a pretence of ruling through the old republican
forms. In 1449 Cosmo's son Lorenzo was born and
lived to earn the title of "the Magnificent."

Lorenzo lived in princely style and his lavish pat-
ronage of the arts attracted about him most of the
great figures of his time into a veritable court of
talent. He was a man of no mean talent himself and

wrote vivacious prose as well as excellent poetry. Indeed, he was not above singing carnival songs of his own composition in the public streets and these were not less appreciated because they were often indecent.

But though Lorenzo busied himself less about his business than his father and grandfather had done, the reputation of the banking house of the Medici continued to mount so high that it was recognized all over Europe. The standing of the Medici may be gauged from the fact that when Edward of England invaded France in 1475 and was bought off by Louis XI on the promise of 50,000 crowns a year for a hundred years, it was stipulated that the Bank of the Medici should be made surety for the continued payment of the indemnity. In other words, Louis XI was to establish a trust fund with them for the period of a century. Other events prevented the fulfilment of this agreement but it illustrates the enormous prestige of the Florentine Magnifico.

After Lorenzo another branch of the family carried the name to further fame and into the papacy itself, but it was not essentially as financiers that they prospered. Two centuries after Lorenzo's death the family had withdrawn from all direct connection with banking.

To-day the only survival of the famous Bank of the Medici is the familiar sign of the three golden balls

[78]

displayed above pawnbroking establishments, an adaptation from the six red balls on the gold field of the Medici shield and the guild shield with its red field strewn with eleven gold florins.

"BY doing good with his money, a man as it were stamps the image of God upon it, and makes both pass current in the merchandise of Heaven."

REV. E. RUTLEDGE.

CHAPTER VIII

FINANCES OF BARCELONA

IF one wished to be fanciful he might say that the Gods had assured Barcelona of a fortunate future. For there is a tradition that Hercules founded the city four hundred years before Romulus had thought of building Rome.

However that may be, the origin of Barcelona is ancient enough. It seems to have been established during the Carthaginian supremacy in Spain by Hamilcar Barca, father of Hannibal, who was to come nearer the conquest of Rome than any of the ancients. The city at that time was called Barcina, after its founder, and so derives its present name which was officially confirmed when the Bishopric of Barcelona was created in 343 A. D.

After the Roman power was withdrawn from Faventia, as the city was known for a time, it underwent a number of vicissitudes and fell before the Moorish invasion in 713. It was probably shortly after this that the Jews who later played an important part in the economic life of the town, became prominent. The Christians, aided by Charlemagne, recaptured Barcelona in 788. Thenceforth, until the union of

[81]

Catalonia with Aragon in 1149, it was nominally ruled by the counts of Catalonia, who claimed to be independent.

Through all this time the superb situation of Barcelona had constantly tended to make it an important city and eventually it became supreme on the eastern coast of Spain. As early as 1227 the Barcelonian fleet was so numerous that it was decreed these ships should monopolize the trade with Egypt and Barbary.

Most important among the industries of the city was woollen manufacture. This must have been organized before 1257 because there is a record that the wool dyers had a guild at that date. In 1258 the great municipal council numbered one hundred and fourteen representatives of the various trades. Among them were six cloth merchants, nine wool dealers, and four cotton spinners. And to show that banking, even at that time, was looked on as an essential vocation, there were four money changers.

Barcelona lies at the foot of Mount Monjuich. In Roman times this elevation was known as the Mount of Jove but in the Middle Ages it was called Mons Judacius and seems to have been set aside entirely as a Jewish quarter. Therefore, it is quite natural to find a Jew as the first famous financier of Barcelona.

This was Benveniste de Porta, a man of wide rep-

[82]

SETTLEMENT OF ACCOUNTS BY MEDIEVAL GUILD—1466

utation in his day. In 1257 he had become a backer
of royalty, for the records show that on December
seventeenth of that year he advanced 3,863 sueldos
to King James I of Aragon. The loan was secured
and was to be collected from the dues of his bailiwick.

Repeatedly during the next few years he acted as
the King's financier. In January, 1258, for example, he received the right to dispose of the taxes
of Barcelona and Gerona for two years. Again, in
return for a loan of 200,000 sueldos to the King, he
was authorized to collect the revenues of Lerida and
other places. On June 12, 1260, King James drew
a draft against him for 5,000 sueldos, which is one of
the earliest references to such a commercial paper.

In 1262 Benveniste advanced 15,221 sueldos to
the account of the Infanta Donna Juana and received in return the dues of Villafranca and twenty
squares of land. This land grant is of peculiar interest and significance as in most places throughout
Christendom the Jews were forbidden to hold land.
King James, however, was a liberal minded ruler,
and to prove it once listened to a debate between a
Christian, a Mohammedan and a Jew.

Benveniste seems to have financed most of the operations in Barcelona at this time. In 1264 he
loaned 15,000 sueldos to the Bishop of Barcelona,
indicating that religious intolerance was rampant on
neither side. Four years later he was again granted

the right to collect the dues of Gerona. All this time the King seems to have regarded him with the most friendly spirit. As a token of his favour James even went so far as to pardon Benveniste's brother for defaming the Christians.

The sheep raisers formed a guild in 1273 which continued an economic factor in the life of the city for hundreds of years. The next year, however, commerce was threatened when trade with the Mohammedans was forbidden. But Barcelona was too near Moslem territory for such a suppression to be entirely effective. About this time, churchly influence also brought about a limit of twenty per cent on interest, which still further turned the money lending business into the hands of the Jews.

During the reign of Pedro III, from 1276 to 1285, Sicily was conquered. This put Aragon into close touch with Italy, as well as Sicily, resulting in the spread of Italian influence into Barcelona itself. During this period the merchants of Barcelona competed with Italy for the trade of the Levant and were among the earliest to establish consuls and factories in distant ports. The celebrated code of maritime law, *Consolato del Mar,* is believed to have been drawn up at Barcelona. The extension of commerce developed the issue of marine insurance at an early date.

Sicily was an island of mixed population and har-

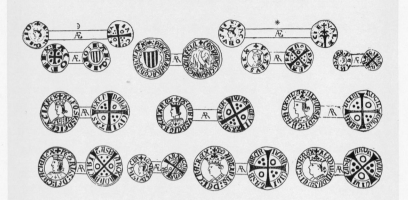

MEDIEVAL COINAGE OF BARCELONA. SOME OF THESE
COINS WERE ISSUED BY JAMES I OF ARAGON

bored Greeks and Mohammedans as well as Italians. Sericulture had long been introduced there and after Pedro's conquest silk manufacture spread to Aragon and other Spanish provinces. But wool remained the great staple of manufacture. By that time the woollen guild was importing wool from England and sending back shipments of finished cloth not only to Britain but also to many other countries. Thus the guild was forced into banking operations for its members as early as 1349. An agent in England could pay a bill there with a draft drawn on the guild, while the guild paper was generally accepted in the cities of Spain and Italy.

In importing wool from England the guild acted as buyer for its various members and in disposing of goods abroad exercised a similar general sales function. Members could also borrow from the guild when necessary. They were not expected to pay interest but were required to give pledges unless the loan was so small that their ability to repay was unquestioned.

Throughout western Europe there were riots against the Jews toward the end of the Fourteenth Century. Superstitious charges that the Jews had introduced the Black Death, or pestilence, which again and again ravaged the most populous communities, were at the bottom of these uprisings. In one such riot at Barcelona, in 1391, the Jewish quarter

was virtually wiped out and many Jewish money
lenders were driven from the city.

This left a void which the thriving commerce of
the city compelled the citizens to fill. Acting on the
example of the drapers' guild and of some of the
Italian cities, the municipality thereupon established
the Bank of Barcelona as an official institution.

This bank received deposits and served as a medium of exchange, issuing drafts and accepting
drafts drawn upon it. Unlike the drapers' guild it
was open to every one, including not merely the citizens of Barcelona and Aragon, but all foreigners as
well. Foreigners were no doubt admitted to help
solve the problem of exchange of money which had
become almost inextricably complex. Barcelona
maintained commercial relations with Aragon, Cas-
tile, France, Mohammedan Spain, Sicily and various
cities in Italy and all of these issued distinctive coin-
ages of their own.

Barcelona always remained proud of her position
as a commercial city and fostered her trade and
manufacture in every way. Business there was
never regarded as degrading as it was in many other
Spanish cities. The municipality was controlled by
the council which was itself composed of representatives of the guilds, as in Florence. Indeed instances
are recorded of some of the lesser nobles renouncing
their rank for the privilege of entering a guild and

[86]

thus establishing their eligibility for municipal offices.

The bank was under the general supervision of the council and so, indirectly, under the control of the guild members whose interests it served. As a result of this close business relationship the bank enjoyed a long and prosperous career.

The discovery of America, which changed the course of commerce throughout the world, affected Barcelona adversely along with the other Mediterranean cities. The cities of the Atlantic coast leaped into sudden importance and Barcelona, though it remains an important industrial centre to this day, never recovered the prestige it enjoyed before Columbus ventured across the western ocean.

"MONEY, the life blood of the nation,
    Corrupts and stagnates in its veins,
Unless a proper circulation
    Its motion and its heat maintains."

DEAN SWIFT.

CHAPTER IX

BIRTH OF THE ENGLISH NATIONAL DEBT AND FOUNDING OF THE BANK OF ENGLAND

THE banker of to-day should find it a curious and interesting diversion to consider how much he owes to the tyrants of the past. It is a commonplace, in all nations derived from English stock, that existing political and legal institutions represent mainly the outgrowth of the struggle of popular rights against the absolutism of kings. To an extent this is also true of banking and currency, as, for instance, the issuance of bank-notes backed by the national governments.

It may fairly be said that such standard features of the modern banking world as the central bank of issue and the national debt come to Americans almost as the direct fruit of the Divine Right of Kings, as this right was perversely applied by two Stuart kings of England, Charles I and Charles II. It was due primarily to the lawlessness and corruption of the second of these kings that England created a national debt and a central bank of issue.

The astonishing crudity of the devices which served

England in place of a banking system in the Middle Ages—almost incredible to the modern mind—made possible the forays of the Stuart kings; and by making these raids possible drove home the necessity of regulating the financial relations between the Government and the people to whom the Government looked for funds with which to carry on.

Charles I set two unfortunate precedents for his immediate successor by twice losing his head. The second loss, as is well known, was fatal to Charles. The first was when he raided the Exchequer or Government Treasury (then housed in the Tower of London), causing a loss to the merchants who had deposited their money there to the amount of £120,-000. This was the precedent which the second Charles followed, on a ten times larger scale, with results probably much more than ten times as far-reaching.

In the careless days of Charles I the methods both of banking and of taxation were crude and confused. For nearly five hundred years before his time the Mint had been a place of deposit for the merchants. Because of the worn condition of the coins, which made them of unequal value, the officials weighed each man's deposit and recorded the amount of the deposit by notches on a stick, which afterwards served as ledger and pass-book. According to Sir John Lubbock, president of the Bankers' Institute

Castrum Royale Londinense   vulgo   the TOWER

IN THE MIDDLE AGES THE ROYAL MINT OCCUPIED A PORTION OF THE
TOWER OF LONDON

of London in 1879, it was not until 1826 that the old wooden tallies entirely passed out of use in England. "The tally," says Sir John, "was a willow stick about five feet long, an inch in depth and thickness, with the four sides roughly squared."

The amount of the deposit was recorded by means of notches on one side of the tally stick, and a description inscribed on the two sides adjoining the notched side. The tally stick was then split in half through the notches, one half going to the depositor, the other half being retained by the bank as its record.

Cromwell, who sanctioned the beheading of Charles I, and who ruled England as "Protector," had a hand in devising the effective and productive system of monthly taxes which enabled the Parliamentary Government to get through periods of great difficulty. This new system was largely continued under the second Charles.

But Cromwell, like the king before him, had to take in his pocket Parliament's authorization for a loan and dicker with the money lenders when in need of funds, the security offered being repayment out of the proceeds of the authorized tax-levy. By this time the former money-lending supremacy of the Jews had passed to the goldsmiths who came to England from Lombardy, and who have left their own monument in modern London in the name of Lombard Street—the Wall Street of the British capital.

[91]

Following the raid of Charles I on the Exchequer, the confidence of the merchants in government depositories began to weaken and they gradually turned to the goldsmiths' strong boxes for a safer depository for their funds. On short time deposits, the goldsmiths levied a small charge for the accommodation; but they paid as high as six per cent interest on deposits placed with them definitely for a year or more.

The charge they made for loans to the Government was generally eight per cent, leaving for themselves, as bankers, a profit of two per cent.

In January, 1672, when the Mint contained some £1,328,000 of bankers' funds advanced to the Government, Charles II acted on the precedent set by his father. In the pay of the King of France, and conspiring against England's safety, he had promised by way of repayment to produce a war between England and Holland. Like many another spendthrift he ran out of funds and, losing his head almost as completely as his father had done, executed his most lamentable raid upon the Mint, seized the funds, and closed the Exchequer, prohibiting its reopening in order to prevent the merchants from cashing their tallies. This famous raid has been known in history ever since as "The Stop of the Exchequer."

This seizure proved to be a serious matter for all concerned. The money, though advanced by the bankers to the Government, represented the fortunes of some ten thousand individuals who had entrusted their funds to the goldsmiths. The bankruptcy and ruin which followed Charles' raid was therefore widespread, and so disastrous that an attempt was made at partial reparation,—an attempt which resulted in the birth of the national debt of England. Charles, in his proclamation closing the Exchequer, declared that the money he had taken would be retained for only a year, but this promise, like most he made, was not kept. The Government paid six per cent interest on the seized funds for six years, from 1677 to 1683, after which all interest payments ceased. No interest was paid during the following short reign of James II, and it was not until another revolution had put William of Orange on the British throne that real reparation came into sight.

An attempt by the Government's creditors to get restitution by action through the courts at first came to nothing since it was ruled that Charles II, and not the Government headed by William, had made the seizure. Years later the House of Lords upset the court decision and partial restitution was made.

Before the end of the litigation was in sight a plan of settlement, based on the creation of a regular Government debt and a bank of issue, was put before Parliament by an obscure Scotchman named William Patterson, who was backed in his efforts by a number of rich London merchants. Taking advantage of

[93]

the Government's need for money, Patterson, in 1692, offered a plan whereby the creditors or their assignees would forego the interest on £1,340,000 owed them, and would advance another sum equal to their principal if six per cent should be secured by act of Parliament, and the bills of the company be made legal tender up to the total amount. Parliament objected to the legal tender feature and nothing was concluded for a year or more.

The plan was revived, however, by Charles Montagu, Lord of the Treasury, who sent for Patterson, to whose assistance later came the astute Michael Godfrey. A loan to the Government of £2,000,000 at seven per cent interest was contemplated at this meeting, but the low rate of interest seemed so preposterous to royal ministers accustomed to waste nearly half the proceeds of a loan in extravagant commissions, that they turned from Patterson's plan to other ways and means.

Two years later the Patterson-Godfrey plan, revised, was carried through a scantily attended session of Parliament as a rider to the Ways and Means Bill. It emerged May 4, 1694, as the charter of "The Governor and Company of the Bank of England." Under the terms of this charter the company was allowed to lend the Government £1,200,000, was authorized to issue notes, deal in bullion, and to make advances on merchandise. Because the bill to which

ENGLISH OFFICERS RECEIVING AND WEIGHING COIN
AT THE EXCHEQUER, A.D. 1130—1174

the Bank rider was attached levied tunnage duties, the Bank itself was long known as "The Tunnage Bank."

Thus England acquired a national debt and a central bank of issue—unforeseeable fruits of the tyranny of the Stuart kings.

"GET all you can without hurting your soul, your body, or your neighbor. Save all you can, cutting off every needless expense. Give all you can. Be glad to give, and ready to distribute; laying up in store for yourselves a good foundation against the time to come, that ye may attain eternal life."

JOHN WESLEY.

CHAPTER X

THE AMSTERDAM BOURSE IN THE SEVENTEENTH CENTURY

ON August 14, 1597 the somewhat sedate streets of Amsterdam suddenly began to echo to the sound of bells ringing in mad excitement. In no time at all a crowd of burghers had gathered at the waterfront, overjoyed at the spectacle they witnessed there. Four Dutch ships, absent more than two years, had returned triumphantly from the Spice Islands of the far-away Indies.

But there was a sober note in the triumph. The little fleet, backed largely by the money of the local merchants, had set out manned by two hundred and fifty men. Only ninety-four of them came back, and these after incredible hardships. But they had successfully defied the power of Spain which, in closing the ports of her then dependency, Portugal, to all Dutch traders, had threatened the very existence of the mercantile navy of the Netherlands.

That memorable voyage marked the metamorphosis of the Dutch from European into World traders. From various ports of Zeeland and Hol-

[97]

land eighty vessels sailed the following year to America, Africa and India. In 1602 the celebrated Dutch East India Company was organized under a charter granted by the States-General with a subscribed capital of 6,000,000 guilders. Within six years this company sent out forty-six ships armed for war, if necessary, and as thoroughly equipped for trade. Holland had begun to take her position as a world power.

Commerce, developing so rapidly, was naturally in confusion. Amsterdam, long a city of importance, had suddenly grown to be a great centre of international trade. It was overrun with foreigners. Its imports and exports reached staggering figures. Indeed, it was the main transfer port between north and south.

The money current in the city flowed in from many lands. It was worn with constant use and where it had not lost weight from long service it was clipped by sharpers. The bulk of it was worth from ten to fifteen per cent less than the new coinage from the mint. This was one of the potent reasons which led to the establishment of the Bank of Amsterdam. It was also urgently necessary to ease the payment of foreign bills of exchange and most of the merchants also desired to avoid the inconvenience of making their payments in actual coin.

Therefore in 1609 the city itself established the

THE AMSTERDAM BOURSE IN THE SEVENTEENTH CENTURY

bank.   It belonged to the city, its credit was guarded by the city, the cost of management was undertaken by the city and if there were any profits they accrued to the city.   At a glance, this has the look of an advanced enterprise in municipal ownership.

Yet the old Bank of Amsterdam is of peculiar interest to-day because it was in many ways so primitive and because it was based on principles so different from those which regulate modern banks.   Its deposits, for example, were presumed always to be equal to its liabilities.   It was not intended as a loan bank at all but as a convenience in commercial exchange.

The institution accepted foreign and domestic coin at its actual value by weight and fineness.   This was credited on the books and the depositor was given both a credit slip and a receipt for the coin each of which was used independently as commercial paper. Gold and silver bullion was received on the same basis.   Both coin and bullion, however, were credited at about five per cent below the mint value.

The bank exacted an additional charge for the storage of bullion if it remained in the vaults more than six months.   For gold this charge was one half of one per cent and for silver one quarter of one per cent.   It was considered more difficult to test the fineness of gold and the risk involved in guarding it was held to be greater.   If coin was left in the bank

[99]

for a period beyond six months the same charge as that for silver bullion was required. Obviously, a considerable part of the bank's income was derived from these charges, though the canny founders had not neglected other sources of profit.

Under the law all monies received and paid, amounting to more than 600 guilders, had to be cleared through the bank and this limit was later reduced to 300 guilders. Bills of exchange, to be legal, had likewise to be paid through the bank. The law was framed to prevent fraud, to provide legal records and to assure safety in the handling of funds.

Perhaps it was merely an incidental consideration that the business of the bank would be enormously extended. However, for each of these multitudinous transactions the institution received not less than two stivers, or four cents. If the transfer fell below 300 guilders the charge was tripled. The results were as profitable as a government stamp tax on all commercial paper.

Another source of profit lay in the multiplication of accounts. Every new depositor was charged ten guilders, or four dollars, and every new account started by him yielded another three guilders. Each deposit was regarded as a separate account and might be negotiated from merchant to merchant for many years. Under the Dutch system the deposit was the

[100]

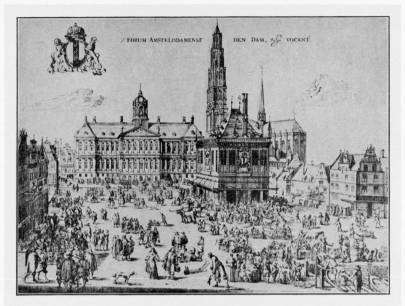

THE FORUM, AMSTERDAM——EARLY EIGHTEENTH CENTURY

unit whereas to-day the individual is usually regarded as the unit.

Certain specific penalties enforced by the management also added to the profit of the bank.

If bullion was not withdrawn within six months after the deposit, or if a new storage charge was not paid, it was supposed to revert to the bank. As a matter of fact bullion was seldom forfeited and storage payments on it often ran over long periods. If a depositor failed to balance his account every six months he was fined twenty-five guilders, or ten dollars.

The profits of the bank, though substantial, varied enormously from year to year. The exact figures were kept secret. But according to old city records of income the profits ran anywhere from 25,000 to 300,000 guilders, and might jump or drop as much as 100,000 guilders from one year to the next. Nevertheless, this was doing very well as the bank was supposed to make no loans to individuals and had not that profitable field to exploit.

The Bank of Amsterdam was under the direction of the four ruling burgomasters of the city, who were changed each year. Every year just before the bank was handed over to the new burgomasters a balance was struck and the transfer was attended by solemn ceremonies. However, the actual figures were not made public.

In 1672, when Louis XIV captured Utrecht there was a run on the bank but it met all demands promptly. Some of the coin paid out at that time had evidently been lying in the vaults of the bank since it had been founded.

Yet perhaps even then all was not as serene as it seemed. Or possibly the following century developed a looser management. At all events when the French captured Amsterdam in 1795 and seized the bank a balance was taken which revealed that the deposits were far below what the receipt book called for. It developed that money had been loaned to Holland, West Friesland, the City of Amsterdam and the Dutch East India Company. How these loans could have been kept secret from one administration to another, with the four burgomasters changed every year, and in the midst of bitter party politics, is a mystery. It must be assumed that the true condition of the bank was considered a state secret outside the realm of internal politics.

Though the city managed to pay the depositors in full before 1802 these revelations had hopelessly ruined the credit of the bank and it soon ceased to exist. Through other means, however, Amsterdam managed to maintain her financial supremacy until it passed to London during the Napoleonic wars.

NATHAN ROTHSCHILD
Founder of the Famous House of The Rothschilds.

CHAPTER XI

RISE OF THE ROTHSCHILDS

LOST in the obscurity of the humble, somewhere in the second quarter of the "excellent, indispensable Eighteenth Century," a Jewish pedlar, Amschel Moses Bauer, decided to settle down at Frankfort, Germany. He had hawked his goods about at Hanover and countless country fairs and he was tired.

The restlessness that was already in men's minds, and was later to set all Europe in flames, had not yet ripened. Bauer opened a little shop in the Judenstrasse. Over his door, as a sign, he swung a red shield. From that house, named from that modest shield, sprang the greatest firm of international bankers of the next century—until our own day the most powerful family of money lenders the world has known.

Bauer had a son, Maier Amschel, the apple of his eye. Maier was a smart boy, and studious. His father, in a wild flight of ambition, decided to make him a rabbi and sent him to the Talmud school at Furth. But in 1754, when Maier was only eleven years old, Moses Bauer died. The boy had to go to work. Eventually he managed to get a clerkship in

[103]

the Oppenheimer bank at Hanover and after a number of years became a junior partner. Yet his mind turned back to Frankfort. Returning, he set up there as a banker in his own right. As a filial gesture he bought the little house with the red shield and assumed the name "red shield" himself—the first of the Rothschilds.

As a boy at Furth, Maier had developed an interest in ancient coins and medals. As a banker he made this interest rather a hobby. This hobby resulted in a contact which influenced his own fortune and that of many others.

Chief of the local connoisseurs was William, Landgrave of Hanau, afterward Elector of Hesse Cassel. In 1785 the Landgrave and General Estorff were disputing the origin of an old coin when the General suggested Rothschild as an expert.

Arriving on summons, Maier found the two at chess.

"Do you play?" the Landgrave condescended to ask.

"A little," responded Rothschild. "And if I may suggest this move your highness will win the game in three moves."

So it turned out. A decidedly tactful suggestion. The victorious Landgrave turned to his friend. "General," he announced, "This is certainly no fool you have brought me!"

COAT OF ARMS OF THE ROTHSCHILDS,
WHICH INCLUDES THE ORIGINAL
RED SHIELD IN THE CENTER

And he, in his turn, was right. From time to time Maier Rothschild bought rare coins for the Landgrave and negotiated bills on London. Like his predecessors, Rothschild's patron was virtually selling soldiers to Great Britain. In 1787, for example, he forwarded 12,000 men and received £80,000 for their services. Thus he became one of the richest men in Europe, often having as much as half a million pounds in his vaults at Cassel, besides substantial deposits in London and Amsterdam. Naturally, this profitable practice made him the enemy of France and when Napoleon crossed the Rhine he was compelled to flee. But he had developed a firm faith in the integrity and shrewdness of Rothschild and left most of his wealth with him. The latter hid £250,-000 in the cellar and sent much more than that to his son Nathan, in London.

This Nathan was not merely the third of Maier's five sons. He was the greatest financial genius of his generation. He was born in 1777 and when he came of age went to England. Manchester attracted him because he saw how three profits could be made in the cotton trade. There, by supplying both materials and dyes and selling the finished product, he expanded his capital from £20,000 to £60,000.

By 1800 he was rich enough to set up as a London banker. Through his father he became within a year the purchasing agent for the Landgrave. Within six years he had attracted considerable attention in the financial world by engineering a loan of 10,000,-000 thalers to Denmark. Indeed, so important was this loan, that Amsterdam never recovered the prestige in financial affairs which London, through Rothschild, had wrested from her.

Naturally, then, when the Landgrave fled, his funds went to Nathan for safe-keeping. Nathan invested them shrewdly and when the time came to make return added five per cent interest. The Landgrave, astonished and delighted, became the firm's greatest advertiser, shouting praises of the House of Rothschild throughout the courts of Europe.

England was now at death grips with Napoleon. Sir Arthur Wellesley, later Duke of Wellington, fighting the power of France in the Spanish peninsula, had drawn numerous orders on the treasury which it could not pay and which were consequently selling at a big discount. Nathan Rothschild had always believed in the ultimate defeat of Napoleon. Acting on that faith, in 1809 he bought up many of these orders and held them as an investment. It was Wellington himself who later said: "Rothschild and I owe something of our .success to knowing what is doing on the other side of the wall."

Meanwhile Rothschild learned that the East India Company wished to sell 100,000 pounds of gold bullion. This he bought, confident that it would soon be needed by the government. His guess was correct. Soon after, the government sent for him and bought his gold to send to Wellesley, who was desperately in need of cash for his army in Portugal. Rothschild himself undertook to deliver it for the sake, as he afterward said, of the extra profit. Not only did he deliver the gold to Wellesley but he sent it boldly through France, the country of the enemy.

By this time Wellesley's treasury orders had been discounted in Portugal and Italy and, in fact, were scattered all over the continent. By 1813 Rothschild had traced most of these down and purchased them for about £700,000. Of course it was necessary that this be done quietly so as not to disturb prices, but Rothschild managed the deal without exciting a ripple.

When two years later Napoleon returned from Elba, England faced another and her greatest crisis.

If Napoleon triumphed Rothschild was ruined. But as usual he was in a strategic position. Adolphe Thiers, the French statesman and financier, tells the story of what happened.

Rothschild was at Ghent. In the next house to his was Louis XVIII of France, driven into exile by Napoleon and now waiting the issue of the field of Waterloo. Through his window Rothschild could see what was taking place in the hall of the King next door. The only news of the battle of Waterloo that

had yet penetrated to the outside world was that
Blucher had been defeated. Yet the watching banker
saw a messenger from the battlefield enter the King's
presence and kneel as though to a reigning sovereign.

This was enough for Rothschild. He felt sure
Napoleon was defeated. He started post haste for
London. Reaching Ostend he found a furious storm
driving across the Channel. Still gambling with fate,
he paid a sailor 2,000 francs in advance to land him
safely in England. In the morning he was able to
take his place in the London stock exchange. None
knew what he knew. What tidings the city had from
Waterloo were bad. Consols were selling at bargain
prices. Rothschild bought all he could lay his hands
on. When the nation finally learned of Wellington's decisive victory the banker's profits amounted
to £1,000,000.

Again and again Rothschild profited by his appreciation of the value of news. He had carrier
pigeons trained to bring him the latest tidings from
Europe and used clipper ships to outrun the ordinary
channels of intelligence of his time. Once he had the
news, his own extraordinary judgment equipped him
to meet and best any competitor.

Rothschild preferred lending money to states
rather than to individuals. In time he became the
fiscal agent of virtually every·civilized government on
the globe, with the exception of Spain and the United

States, from which countries he consistently declined all contracts. His house advanced £18,000,000 to states at war with Napoleon and about £5,000,000 to Prussia after peace had been declared.

All Nathan's four brothers were able bankers and the firm functioned throughout Europe. When Nathan died in 1836 the family rested at the apex of the financial structure of the world. His son Lionel was elected to Parliament but firmly refused to take his seat until the disabilities against Jews had been removed. Honours and titles descended upon the House of Rothschild and to this day it has continued one of the great financial powers of Europe. But always the central office of the firm has been maintained at Frankfort, where it began in the House of the Red Shield.

"HOW a man uses money—makes it, saves it, and spends it—is perhaps one of the best tests of practical wisdom. Although money ought by no means to be regarded as a chief end of man's life, neither is it a trifling matter to be held in philosophic contempt, representing as it does to so large an extent, the means of physical comfort and social well-being."

S. SMILES.

CHAPTER XII

DEVELOPMENT OF BANKING IN
THE LAND OF THE VIKINGS

POPULAR misconception of a name and the very real tradition of terror they left on the coasts of their visitation have combined to create a false notion of the Vikings. Literature has insisted on regarding them as scions of a wild northern royalty, corsairs certainly and perhaps savage princelings. As a matter of fact they were not Vikings at all, but merely Vik-ings—"men of the inlets," or fjords.

As most of the records we have access to were compiled by their Christian and fear-shaken enemies the extremely courageous yet pagan Vikings loom in history chiefly as the deadly scourge of that first, feeble feudalism which was struggling to revive some spark of civilization from the ashes of the Roman Empire. Issuing from their long boats, those dragon ships which were a sign of peril wherever their sails rose above the horizon, they did harry England, Ireland, France, Spain and even the coast of Italy, leaving waste and destruction where they did not actually kill and colonize.

[111]

But the Vikings were much more than pirates. At the height of their vigour their governance embraced the whole northern top of the world, from North America which they discovered and, in some sense settled, hundreds of years before Columbus was born, to the steppes of Russia where Rurik, a Norseman, is the first great historical figure. There is reason to believe the Norsemen sailed up the Great Lakes in America and penetrated as far as Minnesota. In Russia, on the other wing of their far flung exploration, Novgorod is merely the Norse name for "new fort."

All this implies a tremendous maritime energy and an enormous extension of trade, for with the Norsemen trade was a foster sister of the sword. They were a congeries of peoples rather than a nation and in the early mediaeval world some impulse, the cause of which we do not know, inspired them with a cosmic restlessness which brought successive eruptions of their fleets against the coastwise monasteries of France and England and carried them up the Baltic and across the North Atlantic. It is said that the first idea of galleys came to them from the Romans, but the Romans never proved half so venturesome.

Often making their first approach as traders they would return as raiders and finally as conquerors. Thus they came again and again to the shores of France and, sailing up the Seine, at last besieged

Paris. To shake them off it was necessary to cede them the whole province of Neustria which then became Normandy. These Normans, or Norsemen, learned to speak French and within a century conquered England, settled by earlier Norsemen (Angles and Saxons) who had been fighting vigorously, but only half successfully, to keep out their Norse kindred, the Danes.

Throughout all this fierce ferment the Norsemen, or at least that branch of the race which called themselves Swedes, had maintained the city of Visby, on the island of Gottland, as their chief commercial centre. Visby, which retains to-day some of the most interesting mediaeval remains in Europe, is believed to have been one of the most ancient trading centres in the world. There are indications that it was a post of exchange even in the Stone Age when bronze was just being introduced from the valley of the Mediterranean. Old Arabic and even Chinese coins dug up there suggest the almost incredible spread of early Norse commerce.

As the Vikings became Christianized Visby prospered and developed as a thriving commercial republic, sending expeditions eastward into Russia and south through Europe. The whole fur trade of the north centred in the city and pelts were exchanged for the various wares of more luxurious civilizations.

Russia, first developed by the Norsemen, was a

great field for their exploitation. But after the conquest of Russia by the Mongols the trade of Visby was considerably impaired. It also suffered through the rivalry of other Hanseatic towns, which won away much of its southern trade. Finally it was raided by King Valdemar Atterdag of Denmark in 1361 and never afterward managed to recover its prestige.

Even in those early days furs were so much desired that enormous prices were paid for them. Nevertheless silver and gold were scarcely known in the north and the currency was copper. In large amounts copper was heavy and cumbersome. For this reason there developed in Visby a system of written orders for the payment of goods which corresponded somewhat to drafts or checks, except that they were based on furs rather than on specie.

As Visby declined Stockholm became the chief Swedish commercial centre. Trade there was fostered by the Hansa towns of Germany, but their privileges gradually became so oppressive that they were set aside by Gustavus Vasa. Vasa evinced a keen interest in the extension of trade and endeavoured to secure business both in Russia and with the German cities.

Charles XI of Sweden divided the communities into inland and staple towns. These latter were centres for the export of certain staple products, and

COINING OR STAMPING COPPER MONEY IN
SWEDEN IN MEDIEVAL TIMES

it might be that a town would export but one staple and thus be known particularly for that product.

Gustavus Adolphus, that great commander, found time between his campaigns to encourage commerce and business and is reported to have said: "The Kingdom's welfare depends on commerce and shipping."

The first chartered public bank in Sweden was founded in 1656. An excellent account of this is given in the report to Lord Chancellor Hardwicke which has never been published but is treasured in manuscript by the New York Public Library.

Sole rights for the institution were given to John Palmstruch, head of the merchants guild and a prominent miner. The only capital required was whatever cash Palmstruch might have had and the credit of his various mines. The bank was divided into two departments,—the deposit branch which could make no loans, and the loan department which was permitted to lend money on real estate and commodities. Within two years the bank was issuing notes payable on demand, some to order and some to bearer. These were probably the first standard-sized payable-on-demand bank bills ever issued.

The loans of the Palmstruch bank were legally limited to one year and six weeks. The six weeks was perhaps time added to the regular term to permit making a readjustment. The loans were allowed from six to ten per cent interest and as long as the interest was paid that was sufficient to prevent the calling of the loan. There was also a charge for the transportation and storage of securities.

It seems strange that even at that time the coinage of Sweden was based on copper. As the value of copper continued to rise the issuing of bank notes became a losing venture. Another source of loss to the bank was through the extensive forging of notes.

At all events the issue of bills soon exceeded the available funds and during the panic of 1664 the bank ceased to redeem them and they dropped in value even though they were made legal tender by law. In an effort to remedy this situation silver currency was introduced.

Palmstruch himself was subjected to considerable criticism for intermingling the two departments of loan and exchange. The King, however, retained full confidence in him. He was allowed a substantial profit on the coinage of 500,000 hundred-weight of copper, received other presents and marks of esteem and was finally made a noble of the kingdom.

In 1668 the affairs of Palmstruch's bank was partially liquidated and it was merged into the new Riksbank, or Bank of Sweden. Like the earlier institution this also had two departments, one for loans and one for bills of exchange. The loan department

**THE STOCKHOLM BOURSE IN THE MIDDLE OF THE
EIGHTEENTH CENTURY**

This building was the Banking Headquarters in Stockholm in
1782 and today houses one of the oldest Stock Exchanges in the
world. While the exterior has not been altered, the accommo-
dations and equipment are modern in every detail.

received deposits on interest and loaned money for six months or a year on security in hand or on mortgage. In the exchange department, depositors by paying an extra fee had the privilege of drawing on the bank by check. But deposits might be made free if they did not bear interest. Thus the revenues of the King's mines, the taxes and the royal court cash were kept on deposit without interest.

Launched under government auspices, the bank was given a site free and permitted to operate a special paper mill for the manufacture of bank notes. This government favour injured the business of the private money changers and bankers and they started slanderous rumours regarding the conduct of the institution causing a run on the bank, which was promptly halted by a royal proclamation denouncing these misrepresentations.

At first the Bank of Sweden was prohibited from issuing notes, but in 1701 the state deputies decided on a note issue as a separate section of the exchange department. The notes were made transferable but only by written indorsement. Nineteen years later these notes were actually at a premium, possibly because of their great convenience in business. The currency was still on a standard of copper which was, in most cases, too bulky for transfer.

About 1717 Charles XII drew heavily against the funds of the bank, to such an extent indeed, that its

[117]

credit was impaired. But strangely enough, the exactions of Baron Goetz, who was afterward beheaded, proved of benefit to the bank. He demanded that the people deliver their gold and silver for copper checks, or tokens of coin, and they hurried to deposit their specie in the bank. Goetz sought to influence the King to seize these funds, but His Majesty refused and in consequence the bank acquired a great reputation for security.

This was lost, however, in 1740 when government loans had forced the issue of unprotected notes until the liabilities reached about thirteen times the coin reserve. By 1750 the notes had declined in value and in 1776 a readjustment was necessary by which the old notes were redeemed at fifty per cent of their face value. The redemption was not by specie but merely by new transferable notes based on silver.

By this time the finances of Sweden had come a long way from the old fur currency of the Vikings and the rest is merely a phase of modern financial history.

THE OFFICIAL BURNING OF THE ASSIGNATS IN PARIS
END OF EIGHTEENTH CENTURY

CHAPTER XIII

FINANCES OF THE FRENCH REVOLUTION

IN one sense the French Revolution was a great bankruptcy. It was the outcome of bankruptcy and it resulted in bankruptcy. Therefore it represents the one period—and the most violent period—in the ferment of modern civilization when banking was virtually suspended.

The beginning, progress and culmination of that vast cataclysm we call the Revolution may be summed up in three historic epigrams. The first is the slogan under which that magnificent monarch, Louis XIV, governed: "The state, it is I." The second is the prophecy of his successor, Louis XV: "After me the Deluge." And the third is that ferocious reply of Danton's to armed threats against the Republic: "The kings of Europe would challenge us. We throw them the head of a king."

It was the grandiose designs of Louis XIV, successful enough at first but all at last winding into a weary futility, which bled France white and eventually resulted in the loss of the head of Louis XVI. The monarchy was exacting in its demands far beyond the taxable capacity of the country. The na-

[119]

tion, or at least its favoured few, consumed far beyond its power of production. A tower of luxury and privilege had been built on a foundation of misery and poverty. Meanwhile the Encyclopaedists and the Physiocrats wrote and preached assiduously, hoping to philosophize and teach the coming generation. In reality they sowed in men's minds those explosive seeds which were finally to blow the whole social and political structure to atoms.

But in the beginning the Revolution had merely the aspect of a fiscal reform.

Toward the end of the reign of Louis XVI all those questionable shifts to raise money which so pleased and satisfied his queen, Marie Antoinette, had failed. The financial condition of the government was desperate. The national debt amounted to 6,000,000,000 livres, or about $1,200,000,000. There was a yearly deficit of 150,000,000 livres which seemed to have become static.

Underlying all this was a tax system inexcusably unjust. The nobles, who held title to one-third of France, and the clergy, who controlled one-fifth, paid no land tax whatever. This left a grossly disproportionate share to be paid by the common people, or Third Estate. The people also paid a tithe, or income tax, which had originally been one-tenth of the gross production, but under the exactions of the state had risen to a full quarter.

As a result economic conditions were terrible. Most of the industries had been farmed out as official monoplies. It cost from 3,000 to 5,000 livres to become a master craftsman. The ordinary labourer was only able to earn about a bushel of wheat a week and the skilled workman about half again as much. Piled on top of this were an almost incredible number of legalized corvees, or forced labours due from the peasants to the nobles.

To consider this festering situation the government convoked the States General, a mediaeval institution faintly analogous to the British Parliament, which had not been called for centuries. To the assembled deputies the King delivered a speech urging a reform in the finances.

The Third Estate, or commons, having by far the greater number of votes, promptly took matters into its own hands and organized a national assembly. At its demand the King declared on June 23, 1789, less than two months after the calling of the States General, that there should be no loans or taxes without the consent of the deputies. In so short a time France had changed from an absolute into a conditional monarchy. Necker proposed a tax of twenty-five per cent, and it was carried, but even this was wholly inadequate to the need of the country.

On October tenth, Talleyrand took the first great step toward what was to end in a social revolution.

ments and the nominal purchasers in too many cases cut down the timber, got rid of the furnishings, disposed of everything else movable and simply defaulted on the subsequent payments. Perhaps the only beneficial result flowing from the financial reforms of the Constituent Assembly was the abolition of inequitable taxes and the detested corvees.

But even these were hastily abolished before other and better sources of income had been developed. As a result, the legislative assembly which convened October 14, 1791, was obliged to issue 3,300,000,000 livres more in assignats within the next seven months. Such enormous issues could have but one effect. Value began to evaporate from the assignats. During the year 1792 they depreciated from seventy-two to fifty-one per cent of their face value.

On January 25, 1793, King Louis XVI was guillotined. War with most of the rest of Europe followed as a matter of course. Driven on by the need of financing its campaigns, the new republic once more resorted to an issue of assignats. The consequent drop in their value was as sudden as it was irretrievable. By July they had reached twenty-three to the hundred.

The Convention had been responsible for the issue of 7,274,000,000 of assignats. But the Directory, infected by a kind of frantic insanity to raise money, limited the issue of assignats only by the capacity of